Steve Stephenson
UNBEATEN
INNINGS

HANSIB

First published in Great Britain by Hansib Publications in 2022

Hansib Publications Limited
76 High Street, Hertford, SG14 3WY

info@hansibpublications.com
www.hansibpublications.com

ISBN 978-1-912662-54-8
ISBN 978-1-912662-55-5 (Kindle)
ISBN 978-1-912662-56-2 (ePub)

A CIP catalogue record for this book
is available from the British Library

Design & Production by Hansib Publications Ltd

Printed in Great Britain

"Steve has been involved professionally in community development, local government administration and policy development and social and community activism over several decades. His wealth of considerable relevant experiences qualifies him to write expertly on these matters. He has earned his credibility and respect from unstinting, selfless and dedicated work. Of most significance in recent time, is the role adopted by Steve in providing support to others in leadership positions, using his wealth of experience to provide expert advice on decision-making matters, guiding victims of discrimination to secure just outcomes and being a role model for many vulnerable young people in deprived communities."

HERMAN OUSELEY / LORD OUSELEY

"I've known Steve for many years now, and since I've known him, he has not just been committed to flying the flag for cricket, but for using cricket as a vehicle to support and empower the inner city youths and the community at large. He has been dogged, determined and forthright in his quest for improving the lot of the West Indian community, and I know this book will be an inspiration for everyone!"

JOHN BARNES MBE, FORMER PROFESSIONAL FOOTBALLER

"We know of the great cricketers who play on the field, but the world doesn't always get to see some of the great people who make their contribution off the field. We want to again thank Steve for what he has done and will continue to do for the cricketers, the game of cricket and the people of the West Indies."

CHRIS GAYLE, WEST INDIES CRICKETER

"In my several decades as a reporter of West Indies cricket in the UK and the Caribbean, I have known Steve Stephenson as the 'go to' man for help and information on every aspect of the game, from club to international level. His record on promoting charity games and events, awards dinners, hands-on assistance to teams and individuals, with an eye to the future and a mind on the past, is exceptional. He is the indispensable 'Mr West Indies Cricket UK'."

CLAYTON GOODWIN, JOURNALIST

This book is dedicated to my wife, Pamela, and our daughters, Andrea and Simone, whose understanding and sacrifices made it possible for me to do my work.

Acknowledgements

THE FOLLOWING INDIVIDUALS HAVE SUPPORTED and worked with me over many years at different times and places in local government, in the community, and in my voluntary and charity work. I am both inspired by and indebted to them as many of my painstaking and arduous community events would not have been possible without their blessing, hard work and support. The majority of them also spoke out against racial inequalities before the 2020 Black Lives Matter protests, when it was not popular to do so. I have the utmost respect for this group of people. A few of those listed have not worked directly with me, but they are mentioned because they are positive role models who have inspired many, including myself.

BEDFORD: Sylvia Beckford, Carl Bernard, Des Clarke, Cllr Randolph Charles, Murna Eubanks, Nesta Rogers, Stephanie Grant, Delroy and Nadine Solomon, Cleveland Hudson, Glasford Irving, Harvey Stephenson.

BIRMINGHAM: Dr Carver Anderson, Valdez Allen, Steve Batchelor, Basil Clarke, Ben Cunningham, Rosemary Campbell, Bernard Lewis, Tony Kelly, Trevor McIntosh, Stedman Wallen, Beanie Brown, Maxie Hayles, Garnet Stephenson, Monica Coke, Lloyd Blake, Clifton Folkes, EJ Harris, Neville Moore, Erroll Simms.

BRISTOL: Errol Ballin, Hilary Banks, Jean Bowen, Amirah Cole, Asher Craig, Ayannah Griffiths, Mayor Marvin Rees, Ras Judah Abundi, Patrick Langley, James Pearson, Trevor Samuels, Jendayi Serwah, Clifford Windeth, Babs

Williams, Cliff Young, Winston Young, Batook Pandya, Alex Raikes, Sado Jirde.

JAMAICA: Aloun Assamba, Brian Breese, Gareth Breese, Courtney Francis, Maurice Foster, Gary Herbine, Derrick Heaven, Dorothy Hopkins, Joan McLeod, Easton McMorris, Ruddy Marzouca, Michael Holding, Philip Trenchfield, Jamaica Defence Force (JDF) Brigadier Roderick Williams, Lieutenant Colonel Kirk Johnson and Major Marlon Kennedy, Richard Staple, Dr Rohan Willis.

JAMAICAN DIASPORA UK BOARD: Dr Kevin Brown, Jennifer Blake, Fitzroy Grant, Elizabeth Mullings, Bettina Wallace, and the other board members.

LONDON: Keith Van Anderson ('The Pipe Man'), Delores Cooper, Frank Gibson, Professor Gus John, Lee Jasper, Tony Leslie, Al Hamilton, Rudi Page, Paulette Simpson, Virrol Liverpool, Rodney Hinds, George Ruddock, Florence Harris, Lord Herman Ouseley, Baroness Doreen Lawrence, Neville Lawrence, Seth Ramocan, Vivienne Siva.

LUTON: Bernard Abbey, Godfrey Arthur, Bishop Alvin Blake, Bob Baker, Newton (Beanie) Bernard, Harry and Curla Bruce, Melvin Ellis, Claude and Geraldine Burton, Carl Campbell, Cllr Gilbert Campbell, Valerie Grant, Dr Richard Grant, Terry Gooding, Cecil Harrison, Franklin Hunter, Hannibal Kandekore, Veronica Joseph, Noel Lewis, Oswald Lewis, Cllr Jim Thakoordin, Patrick Markland, Lorna Markland, Lawrence Palmer, Elwood Smith, Henry Rhiney, Dotlyn McCarthy Paul, Francis Reid, Paulette Rose, Leslie Scafe, Pearl Stephenson, Mark Stephenson, Valerie Taylor, Eileen Williams, Cllr Desaline Stewart, Cllr Neville White, Selwyn Johnette.

MANCHESTER: Carlyle Stuart.

MILTON KEYNES: Wain McIntosh, Karl Delisser

NORTHAMPTONSHIRE: Dr Orville Brown, Bert Cuff, Paul Crofts, Sylvia Erskine, Cllr Ulric Gravesande, Mike Prescod, Clyde Lesley, Olive Robinson, Jacques Williams, Billy Walker, Ajona Roy, Sika Smith, Andrea and Simone Stephenson, Jenny Sebastian, Pratima Dattani.

SCOTLAND: Cllr Graham Campbell, Professor Geoffrey Henry Palmer.

SPORTS AND ENTERTAINMENT: Thanks to the support of the following, I have been able to raise money for various charitable causes by working with cricketers: Chris Gayle, Clive Lloyd, Sir Curtley Ambrose, Brian Lara, Darren Powell, David Capel, Courtney Walsh, Jimmy Adams, Richie Richardson, Sir Vivian Richards, Gordon Greenidge, Alvin Kallicharan, Deryck Murray, Collis King, Phil Simmons, Corey Collymore, Franklyn Rose, David Ripley, Devon Malcolm, Chris Lewis, Ron and Dean Headley, John Maynard (the Dentist), John Holder, the Test umpire, the West Indies cricket team, Nehemiah Perry.

I have also received support from Black footballers like John Barnes, Brendon Batson, Cyrille Regis, Paul Elliott, Mark Walters, Ricky Hill, Fitzroy Simpson. Other celebrities include Rudolph Walker, Donna Croll, Jodie Hanson.

SWINDON: Nathan Ajole, George Carty, Colin Cole, Sharon Cheesely, Seniz Ismet, Judy Henry, Gloria Morgan, Pamela Stephenson.

WOLVERHAMPTON: Michael Bigby, Joey Smith, Enrico Stennett.

VICTORIA MUTUAL CARIBBEAN CUP CRICKET NATIONAL COMPETITION COMMITTEE UK: Guy Reid-Bailey, Trevor Davis, Ahmed Kazi, Eaton Gordon, Denton Thomas, Errol Simms, Dr Beverley Lindsay, Charles Robinson, Leroy Thomas, Trevor Taylor.

I would like to give a special mention and personal thanks to the following individuals who gave permission to include their photographs in this book: West Indies Test cricketers Chris Gayle, Sir Curtly Ambrose, Michael Holding, Sir Vivian Richards, Courtney Walsh; footballers Ricky Hill, Cyrille Regis; actor Rudolph Walker, and Lord Herman Ouseley.

My thanks are also due to Tony Kelly and Andrea Stephenson for their patience and proof reading skills; and to Arif Ali and Kash Ali of Hansib Publications for publishing this book.

Contents

Prologue

Steve Stephenson, MBE, a veteran community and equality and human rights activist is a remarkable individual who amongst other things is a pioneer in community development in Britain. Steve is the former chairman of the Victoria Mutual Caribbean Cricket Cup National Competition in the UK, and I was honorary president. He has supported Jamaican and West Indian cricketers over the past 30 years and put on various functions for West Indies teams when they are in England. He is also the organiser of the Winston Davis Annual Benefit Match, of which I have been captain a few times.

Steve has been very consistent in his support for Jamaican and West Indies cricket and the Caribbean community in the UK over the years. He has managed to bridge the gap from one generation of West Indian cricketers to another, although the contribution he has made to club and league cricketers has not been fully recognised, especially the mentoring and support which contribute to these cricketers becoming responsible adults.

In addition to his commitment to the cricketing world, he has also been involved with charity work with famous footballers. During the period I worked with him, we managed to raise thousands of pounds for various charitable causes, together with the support of his wife Pamela and their two daughters.

Throughout this book, Steve has shown how his lived experience relates to equality and social justice issues, which is very relevant to the current situation in Britain and the Caribbean through the Black Lives Matter protests.

Ambassador Courtney Walsh OJ

Foreword

One of the noteworthy facts of recorded history is that not everyone who has contributed positively to progressive developments in society achieves the public recognition they have earned and deserved. Undoubtedly, there are too many to mention in high profile ways, but their contributions are often unknown and even unappreciated.

It is therefore always eye-opening when someone takes the initiative to record the work of unheralded individuals who are leaders, ground-breakers and change agents in helping society to move forward. One such individual, Steve Stephenson, himself a ground-breaker, has spent most of his adult life paying tribute to the successes of high profile achievers.

His active world has been largely around the fields of community development, public service policy developments, assisting victims of racial discrimination and tackling racism in sport, mainly in cricket and football, two of his passions.

One of his most notable achievements in his book is to pay tribute to the pioneers of Black British football. Of course, he did not attempt to cover all those Black footballers, campaigners and supporters who had been in the struggle for more than a century to tackle racism in British football. However, it does set an agenda for others to emulate in raising awareness about a special group of individuals Steve describes as 'pioneers'. That is the mark of Steve Stephenson. Over the past four decades he has dedicated his life to service which benefits community and race relations.

Steve has been involved professionally in community development, local government administration, policy development, and social and community activism throughout his working life. His wealth of considerable experience qualifies him to write expertly on these matters. He has earned his credibility and respect from unstinting, selfless and dedicated work.

Of most significance in recent time is the role adopted by Steve in providing support to others in leadership positions, using his own experience to provide expert advice on decision-making matters, guiding victims of discrimination to secure just outcomes, and being a role model for many vulnerable young people in deprived communities.

Progress towards a just and fair society for all may have been pedestrian, but nevertheless there has been some headway. Whilst the high-profile pioneers deserve their plaudits, we must never forget the unmentioned, low-profile heroes on the frontline, working day and night amongst deprived communities and who support the positive development of the next generation of young people from all backgrounds.

Steve has given unstinted service to the community through his public and voluntary service. He has also been a pioneer, and along with many other unheralded foot soldiers like himself it is important that their contributions are acknowledged as the passage of time tends to focus on the now and can overlook the past.

Now it is for new pioneers, the current and next generation of trail-blazers to carry the equality and inclusion baton forward. Their contributions will benefit from being knowledgeable about all those who have helped along the way to get us to where we are now. Their impact through their words and actions must contribute positively to make British society better for everyone.

All innings have an end point but for now, Steve, ever the cricketing fanatic, remains not out!

Herman Ouseley / Lord Ouseley

Introduction

The title of this book *Unbeaten Innings* has a double meaning, as when a batsman has finished an innings one hundred 'not out', he has said to have played an 'unbeaten innings'. Steve Stephenson has not only devoted his life to the game of cricket, but has remained unbeaten as a race equality, human rights and community activist over the past 40 years.

I have had the pleasure to work with and support Steve for over 25 years with his sports, charity and community work. During that time I have attended charity cricket matches, dinner and dance events, and helped to recruit foster carers, as well as reading poetry and making presentations at some of his organised gatherings. Steve is also the founder of the Winston Davis Annual Benefit Match.

In 1998, he organised a Tribute to the Pioneers of Black British football in Birmingham which was a ground-breaking and historical event that was attended by over three hundred people, including 30 Black footballers and a galaxy of celebrities from various other fields.

As former Director of the Race Equality & Human Rights Service in Bristol, Steve is an exceptional individual who was a pioneer in community development in the UK. Whilst most people excel in one area, Steve has excelled in many. He has been a social worker, youth and community worker, lecturer, and a sports and charity promoter. In addition, he has supported the Black community in Bedford,

Luton, Birmingham, Northamptonshire, Bristol and Swindon as well as helping people in the Caribbean.

Steve was also manager of the iconic Malcolm X Community Centre in St Pauls, Bristol. He worked at the centre during a particularly difficult period, but always made a positive contribution. He wrote a business plan for the centre, and worked with the committee to help to stop its closure.

Steve has worked as Principal Equalities Officer (Race) for Swindon Borough Council and is the former Chair of Swindon's Race Hate Crime Forum. He is in the *Black Who's Who* and *The Voice* newspaper's list of the 100 most influential Black people in Britain. He was a Director of Milton Keynes Racial Equality Council and was instrumental in saving the REC from closure in 1998. His other key post was as Principal Officer for Ethnic Minorities at Northamptonshire Social Services, where he worked closely with the Home Office on Section 11 grants.

He was one of the first Black lecturers at the Birmingham Polytechnic, now the University of Central England. Steve has lectured widely on equality issues, and has been involved in teaching Black History since 1976, long before Black History Month started in October 1987.

One of his main achievements is in relation to human rights. Steve was directly involved in the freeing of David Anthony Grant who was held 'at Her Majesty's Pleasure' in Jamaica for his involvement in a murder. He was only 14 at the time, and was found guilty along with three adults and spent 18 years in prison. The evidence showed it was a miscarriage of justice. After civil rights groups and an MP failed to get his release, David's mother approached Steve who teamed up with lawyer Rudy Narayan and used his influence to get PJ Patterson, the Prime Minister of Jamaica at that time, to finally free David in 1988.

In 1994, Steve was interviewed by Denise Saul for the *Caribbean Times* newspaper. In her article she wrote the headline, 'The Good Samaritan of the Community', which is a fitting tribute to Steve and his lifetime's work.

What is reflected right throughout this book is Steve and his family's kindness, generosity and humanity towards other human beings. Finally, with the advent of the Black Lives Matter movement, whilst most people in the community 'talked the talk', Steve has surely been shown to have 'walked the walk'.

Rudolph Walker, OBE, CBE

CHAPTER ONE

Kingston, Jamaica

I was born in Bread Lane, Denham Town in Kingston, Jamaica on 10 December 1953 – now celebrated as Human Rights Day. My father was called Harvey Royston Stephenson and my mother's name was Pearl Agatha. I was one of nine children, five of whom were born in Jamaica – Beverlyn who was the eldest, then me, Fred, Garnet and finally Harvey who was the baby of the family.

My grandmother Henrietta Jane Ford, whose married name was Simpson, came from St Elizabeth and was affectionately known as Heti. She had given birth to fourteen children, with two dying as infants and the rest growing to adulthood. When I was young I thought she was white because she had long white hair and used to sit under a mango tree in the front yard. However, I was told by my relatives that we were all brown-skinned Jamaicans, although this did not mean much to me at that time.

One thing that really amused us as youngsters was our given names. Fred's full name was Alfred Riggington Stephenson, Garnet had Kipling as his middle name and Harvey's first name was really Kernel. My first name was Silbourne, which was also unusual. We also had a laugh at our cousin – 'aunt' Eda's son – who was called Winston Churchill Willis. Of course, we were too young to realise that he was named after Britain's wartime prime minister! We used to say that our father must have been drinking Wray and Nephew rum to have given us those names.

However, we found out later when we came to England that he was not a drinker.

My father left for England in 1957 and was one of the generation of people we now call 'the pioneers' or the 'Windrush Generation'. My mother followed him ten years later, by which time my father had moved from London and was living in Luton, Bedfordshire. My younger siblings were subsequently born in England and have the less unusual names of Arlene, Mark, Sandra and David.

My sister Beverlyn was the first to join our parents in 1966. Fred and Harvey followed soon afterwards whilst Garnet and I were the last to make the journey to England. Fred was a very generous young man who worked hard, and he looked after us as best he could. Fred worked for Mr Palmer who was employed by the Gore brothers, a Syrian building company. He was very talented with his hands and always took pride in saying that he did a lot of the tiling in the Citizens Bank in downtown Kingston. However, it seems that he was getting involved with a local gang, so my parents decided to send for him along with Harvey.

One of my earliest memories is when I ran away from my mother's home in downtown Kingston to visit my beloved aunt Edna, who I subsequently grew up with. At that time, it was quite common for the extended family to bring up their relatives' children. I had a relation who visited her aunt for Christmas dinner with her parents when she was a toddler, and never went back home again! She just stayed with her aunt until she went to the United States as an adult. She always referred to her aunt as her mother, despite the fact that her birth mother only lived a few miles away.

Luckily, for us our Aunt Edna and her daughter Eda were kind and generous so both my siblings and myself were well cared for, which was not the experience of many children when their parents left Jamaica to seek a better life in what we were told was the 'Mother Country'. My wife Pamela, for example, was not treated very well by her aunts and to this day she has not forgiven them. She was on her

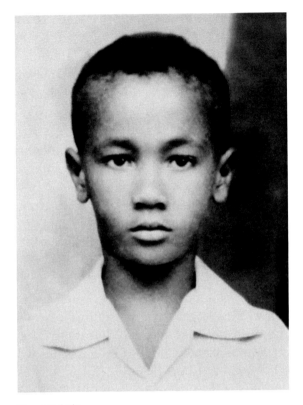

Me, aged six

own, but we were four boys and one sister and in our teens we could stand up for ourselves if anyone tried to take advantage of us. Fortunately we had a lot of other family members who were also good to us.

Eda was actually our first cousin, but because she was an adult when we were growing up we called her 'aunt' Eda out of respect. She had two children of her own who were named Winston Willis and Joan McLeod. This was the same with our cousin Lee Rochester who also helped to look after us before she migrated to England. Lee and her husband Palm (affectionately known as Mr Rochester, another of the original Windrush Generation) become one of my first mentors. The couple raised three talented daughters, Patricia, Emma and Mandy, whom I am really proud of.

We were fortunate to have an uncle named Tom Simpson who was living with us at 23 Deanery Road, Kingston. He had a good job as a property agent for C.G. Plummer, who owned a lot of property in Kingston. Uncle Tom was one of the few men who drove a car in the 1960s. He had an Austin Rover and we were lucky to be taken for drives in the countryside. At Christmas time he would dress up as Santa Claus and gave us presents. He was the father of my three cousins who also lived with us, Angela, Raymond and Michael. Looking back you could say we had a middle class life style compared to many Jamaicans at the time.

I have been very proud of the achievements of some of my family members in Jamaica whose success has been achieved through the combination of education and hard work.

My cousin Winston and his wife Pamela brought up three boys who have grown to be well adjusted men and high achievers because both of their parents valued education. I am especially proud of Rohan Willis who is now a medical doctor. Winston's sister Joan has been equally impressive in her own achievements. When she was born she had a problem with her eyes which has affected her all her life, but she still passed her 'A' levels including Maths, and subsequently got a job with a Canadian bank based in Jamaica. Joan has been with that bank for over forty years. I was really impressed when I visited and spent time at her new home in the area of Orange Grove in Kingston. Their mother, whom I called aunt Eda, would have been so proud of both Joan and her grandson Rohan's achievements.

SCHOOL DAYS

My early years were perhaps the happiest and the best of my life. I first went to Miss Morris's private school in Vineyard Town, and later to Franklin Town primary school, Vauxhall secondary school and Camperdown High school respectively.

At primary school I first heard the expression from teachers to "Learn all you can before you grow old. For learning is better than silver or gold, silver or gold will vanish away but a good education will never decay." Another saying I recall was: "Good better best, never let it rest until your good is better and your better is best."

I attended Vauxhall secondary school with my sister Beverlyn who was always smartly dressed in her school uniform. The teachers at that time were always prepared to go above and beyond the call of duty. One teacher used to collect myself, my brother Garnet and my cousin Raymond and take us to a youth club one evening per week. I recall that I was initially scared of my head teacher D.C. Tavares at Vauxhall school because he once gave me three strikes with the cane for being late. However, one evening he saw me walking to the school gate in the dark, after my practice for the school play. He offered me a lift in his car and took me to my home where he waited until I went through the door before driving off. From that day onwards I came to respect him and was no longer scared because although he was a disciplinarian he had shown that he was also a caring person.

I remember being in Form 8D with a boy named Robbie Shakespeare. One day in class our maths teacher Mrs Robinson said: "Robert William Shakespeare. What a nice name for a bad boy!" Rumour had it that Robbie was going to the notorious Dungle to practise with other musicians near a place called Paradise Street which was by the sea in Kingston. This boy turned out to be Robbie of Sly and Robbie fame. I must admit that I have not seen him since our school days, but the closest I came to meeting him again was during a tour of England when Burning Spear played at the Kingsway Hall in Dunstable, Bedfordshire. I managed to meet up with Winston Rodney, but when I asked if I could speak to Robbie, he told me that Robbie had missed that leg of the tour and was in London.

During the 1960s in Kingston you could go anywhere as a young boy and people would look after you. If we wanted a drink and hung about near a bar one of the men would always buy us a 'soft' drink. I remember a lady whom we called Mrs Happily who was also very kind. I was playing near her house one day during the summer holidays, and she gave me some lunch. I then turned up at her gate almost every day about lunch time and she always would give me some food. If I was playing in my area and I fell over there was always someone who picked me up, brushed me down and sent me on my way. Looking back, I did not know what community spirit meant then, but these kind people definitely saw us as part of their community and always did what they could to help one another.

When school was finished and at the weekend, we boys were able to do just as we pleased. Fortunately, but unfairly for some, we came from a large family. Because of this we had many cousins, mostly girls, who came to stay with us in Kingston. As a result they did all the house work, whilst I and my brothers were left to do whatever we wanted all day long. When we were not playing cricket we spent our time by the sea in Kingston harbour which was still quite clean and unpolluted in the 1960s. We only lived a five-minute walk from the harbour where we not only swam and tried to dive for conchs and catch fish, but also spent a lot of time playing cowboys, pirates and buccaneers.

Black and white television had arrived in Jamaica by that time, and we used to go to a place called Lumber Yard on Windward Road to watch our favourite shows such as *Bonanza*, *Sea Hunt* and the adventures of the British sea captain Francis Drake. We then imitated everything we saw on those TV shows. The fee for entry to Lumber Yard was sixpence, although sometimes we would sneak around the back and the owner would let us watch for free because we were regulars.

I, Harvey, Garnet and our older cousin Winston Willis must have swallowed half the salt water in Kingston harbour learning to swim. We used to go to Barnett and Saguenay beach which was surrounded by a square wooden wall so that people could swim in safety. Winston, who was the oldest, learnt to swim first and he told us that once we learnt to float with a rubber tyre we would be able to swim. We also used to go to Bournemouth beach which had an outdoor swimming pool.

A lady named Mrs Daphne Bedassie, who helped to support me financially when I was at school, worked in the reception at Bournemouth swimming baths and often took me and her son Dirk in to swim for free. However, at other times we all managed to get in without paying. We simply went to a park next door and swam about fifty yards out to sea and then back into the grounds of Bournemouth beach. I think the guards probably used to see us, but as we were only children they did not try to stop us. Mrs Bedassie also worked as a receptionist at the Carib Theatre in Kingston, and I became the envy of my school friends when I was taken to see the premiere of the first James Bond film *Doctor No* which was filmed in Jamaica.

We had two other cousins, Pauline and Dennis Laidley, who came to live with us from the country before migrating to London. Dennis, who was known as Junior, was about the same age as me and he joined us in many of our mischievous activities. Whenever we meet at family gatherings now, he always reminds me of the 'good old days'!

Although I did not take much notice of them at the time, the great Ska band Tommy McCook and the Satellites used to practise upstairs in a large room adjacent to the Bournemouth swimming pool. McCook had learnt to play music at Alpha Boys School where my aunt Edna worked as a cook. He also directed the Supersonics for Duke Reid, and backed many sessions for Bunny Lee with the Revolutionaries at Channel One Studios in the 1970s.

It was years later when people started talking about Jamaican music in England that I realised just how influential the Satellites had been. They played alongside Byron Lee and the Dragonaires at the Syrian club close to where I and my cousin Winston lived with Aunt Edna and her husband Lucien. Byron Lee and the Dragonaires – now known as the Dragonaires after the death of Byron in 2008 – was a Jamaican Ska, Calypso and Soca band that played a crucial pioneering role in bringing Caribbean music to the world. They were chosen to perform in the 1962 James Bond film *Dr No* which brought them to the attention of an international audience. Their 'Dance Hall Soca' hit that was recorded with Admiral Bailey was credited with starting the Ragga-Soca craze of the late 1990s.

CRICKET

My love for sports, especially cricket, developed whilst living with Aunt Edna and her husband Lucien Hopwood. They both worked at a sports club owned by Syrians in Deanery Road in Kingston. In addition to Lucien's other jobs, he used to roll the cricket pitch for weekend matches. As a result I and my cousin Winston, who was a talented left handed batsman, spent a lot of time playing cricket in the field away from the main cricket pitch. We played nearly every day after school until it was dark.

At that time, we made our own cricket balls from the roots of the bamboo plant. However, some of my friends went to Bellevue, the mental health asylum on Windward Road, to buy cricket balls made from white cloth that were sold by the residents who stood at the fence. We called the balls 'mad man balls', but looking back this name was clearly inappropriate. When we went to Manchester in the country we had access to an abundance of lemons and green oranges to play cricket with, so we used the green hard ones for cricket balls.

Back then we made all the toys that we played with. Aside from cricket balls, my cousin Winston Willis taught us to make scooters with two ball bearings, and how to make gigs from the wood of the Lignum Vitae tree which is Jamaica's national flower.

Sometimes school friends would join in with us to make two cricket teams. In those days we had no pads or protection, much less helmets, and I was often hit in the side by the fast bowlers, and also lost a few fingernails. Of course, this did not stop either me or any of my friends!

Later, when we played at school, we were given one pad and a box between us for protection. We used to bat in the one pad and we all shared the box as there was no fear of infections back then. When a batsman was out, he quickly took off the pad and took out the box which protected the genitals. This was simply given a quick wipe and swiftly passed on to the incoming batsman.

When I attended Camperdown High School I had the privilege of playing a few Sunlight Cup cricket matches, and was playing youth cricket during the same period as the great Michael Holding. I remember one match at Kingston College pitch on Elliston Road in particular, as we simply could not cope with his extra pace. I reminded Michael of this, years later, when I met him in England. Although we were not friends in Jamaica I was very proud of the fact that he went on to represent Jamaica and the West Indies, and will never forget his 14 wickets for 149 at the Oval cricket ground in 1985.

Years later Wavell Hinds from Camperdown followed the same path as Michael and also played for the West Indies cricket team.

Camperdown High School was really more renowned for athletics than cricket due to Donald Quarrie, the 200 metres Olympic champion, who had been a pupil there. However, we did also have some very talented cricketers, including Donald's brother Eddie Quarrie, Andy Andrews and Paul Ince. I particularly remember two events relating to these cricketers, one of which had what might be called a direct impact upon me!

Andy's talent was recognised when he was called up to play for Jamaica's under-15 team in Barbados. At that time Andy had a big Afro hairstyle and he was encouraged to cut his hair before he went to the tournament. He did as he was told, but the tour was cancelled and he remained quite upset for a long time afterwards.

Paul Ince was a promising fast bowler whom I believe also went on to represent Jamaica at under-15 levels. Before a game started at Camperdown, I asked Paul if he could bowl a few balls to me. I had no pads on, and did not expect him to bowl so fast, but one of the balls hit me on my shin. This was only about a week before I was due to leave for England in March 1971. My shin was swollen to about the size of half an apple and was brownish red in colour. When I arrived in England I was immediately taken to hospital where a needle was used to drain the blood from the wound, and that was the end of the matter.

WEST INDIES V ENGLAND AT SABINA PARK

In February 1968, when I was nearly fifteen years old, I went to a cricket Test match between the West Indies and England at my beloved Sabina Park. As schoolboys we never used to pay to get into the ground as all we had to do was wait patiently at the back gate and the staff would then let us in. Whenever we were in school uniform the men at the gate would ask us to read something from our school books, and once we read it to them they allowed us free entry.

On this particular day, I was a spectator in the South Camp Road bleachers stand when bottles started to rain down upon the field of play. All of sudden, the police began to fire tear gas under the stand and my eyes started to stream. I had never experienced anything like this before, and I decided to jump over the barbed wire fence to safety. During the process of escaping I received a cut from the wire to the right upper side of my stomach; to this day I still have the scar which is about four inches long. Although it has faded over the years, I still can see it. This minor injury became a 'badge of honour' for me as whenever I was playing cricket in Luton or when there was any discussion about Test matches at Sabina Park I would pull up my shirt to show people the mark.

Of course, I was an innocent bystander caught up in these events.

Crowd trouble started on the fourth day of play when Basil Butcher was correctly given out by umpire Douglas Sang Hue. This was the fifth wicket to fall in the second innings with the West Indies still 28 runs behind.

The police then used tear gas to subdue the crowd. Unfortunately strong winds blew the gas back towards the police, into the commentators' stand and then into the main pavilion, where the Governor-General, Clifford Campbell, and other dignitaries were watching the match. The match then had to be extended by seventy minutes into a sixth day to make up for the lost time. A century by Gary Sobers set England with a target of 159 to win, but the match ended with England on 68-8, still 90 runs behind.

Douglas Sang Hue and Cortez Jordan were the umpires in the second drawn Test of the series. West Indies were bowled out for 143 in their first innings, 233 runs behind England, and were asked to follow-on.

Geoff Smith, the Jamaican Broadcasting Corporation commentator at that game, wrote an article on 7 June 2008 entitled 'Riot, What Riot?' In it, he suggested that the Kingston Test in 1968 is best remembered for the ill-advised use of tear gas by the police to control the crowd. Describing play on the fourth day of the second Test between West Indies and England, E.W. Swanton wrote in the *Daily Telegraph*: "Typing this with more than a whiff of tear gas making things unpleasant in the press box, one is confused by events..."

The trigger had come a few minutes earlier when Basil Butcher had been caught left-handed, low down behind the wicket by Jim Parks off Basil D'Oliveira's bowling from the north end of the ground. Neither Barbadian umpire Cortez Jordan at square leg, nor standing umpire Douglas Sang-Hue from Jamaica needed to signal; Butcher walked immediately when he saw his leg glance fail.

Before David Holford joined Gary Sobers at the wicket one or two bottles and other catering trash had been thrown from the area of the scoreboard in the direction of John Snow at third man. Much abuse was shouted at the batsmen as West Indies, who were following on, were still 25 runs in arrears. Not unknown for his belligerence, Snow advanced towards the crowd appealing for calm. Instead, a greater storm of debris rained down upon him. Colin Cowdrey, England's captain, then strode over in an attempt to placate the spectators. Sobers also walked over to the crowd to try to appeal for calm. But just as it seemed that they had quelled the trouble, matters were taken out of their hands by the local police who hustled across the playing area to confront the protestors. Almost immediately they were followed by the police's mobile reserve wearing white riot helmets and waving long truncheons. These moves proved ineffectual and much 'cussing' – a local term for good-tempered, vocal abuse – developed, encouraging spectators in the South Camp Road bleachers to join in. More bottles rained down on the field of play.

An order was then given for tear gas to be fired into the crowd in the south east bleachers. This caused them to disperse quickly, some incurring minor injuries in the scramble, but the bulk of the gas from the ten or so canisters was blown back at the police themselves. Some of the gas was drawn by the air conditioning units into the media area. As Swanton reported, it was "Most unpleasant".

Following my own injury on the fourth day of play, I did not go back to watch the rest of the Test.

HAILE SELASSIE AND MARTIN LUTHER KING, JR

There are a few significant events that are worthy of mention which both I and my brother Garnet witnessed as young boys growing up in Kingston.

In 1966, we lived on Mountain View Avenue. On the 21st April, Garnet and I were with some friends, standing about in front of Lumber Yard beside a small shop that was near the junction of Mountain View Avenue and Windward Road. Anyone who is familiar with East Kingston will know that after leaving the airport and travelling along the

Palisades Road you pass the cement factory on the right, Rockfort Spa and then Mineral Bath before you get to Windward Road. This was long before the bypass near the sea in Kingston was built.

That day when Emperor Haile Selassie came to Jamaica it was raining heavily. Yet as his plane landed the rain suddenly stopped, and the tarmac was crowded with people who shoved security forces out of the way so that official protocol had to be scrapped. Inside the plane the Emperor waited for half an hour, surprised and overwhelmed by the enthusiastic welcome. Eventually the Emperor requested that a Rastafarian – Mortimer Planno who had previously visited Ethiopia – help him to navigate his way through the throngs of people.

When he finally left the airport, the Emperor travelled in a cavalcade which passed that junction with Windward Road. I saw him standing up straight like a soldier in a khaki uniform in the back of a jeep, and he looked very dignified.

That visit 55 years ago is the stuff of legends, and I heard it retold several times. For Rastafarians it was a visit from a man they consider divine. For newly independent Jamaica it was the visit of an African king predicted by the great Marcus Garvey, who said, "Look to the East for the crowning of a Black King, he is the Redeemer for the days of deliverance are near."

As a young boy I obviously did not realise the importance of the visit to the country or to the Rastafarians, although later in life I recall that the name Mortimer Planno came up in several conversations during my Black History classes at the Starlight Youth Club.

The second event took place after I and my brothers joined a uniformed group called the Air Marines. This was a small group which was outside of the scout movement in Jamaica. It was founded and run by Horlicks Alexander, a very kind and enthusiastic gentleman who lived in a new house in Ellison Flats. I understand that one of his relatives was a Rhodes Scholar, and by Jamaican standards his family were well-off and 'upper-class'.

Alexander was an educated man and a pilot who taught us the Morse code and got us onto ships and small aircraft. The first ship I ever visited was the *HMS Provider* when she was docked in Kingston harbour. Looking back, with no father on the island, it was good to have an adult role model to look up to in addition to my uncles Tom and Noel Simpson.

One day Mr Alexander told us that he had gotten permission from the government for me, Garnett and Raymond to raise both the Jamaican and United States flags at an event taking place in the National Stadium. I was only fifteen years old and did not fully understand the significance of what was about to take place.

Coretta Scott King, the wife of the late Martin Luther King, Jr, was coming to Jamaica for her third visit to accept the first Marcus Garvey prize for human rights. This prize was going to be presented to her on 10th December 1968 at the national stadium by Prime Minister Hugh Shearer. Her visit was just eight months after King had been shot dead by James Earl Ray in Memphis, Tennessee.

After the flag raising ceremony Garnet and I were seated near the royal box. I waved to Coretta and her children, and she waved back. Of course I did not realise or understand that the lady who waved to me was known as the 'First Lady of the Civil Rights Movement'. According to the *Baltimore Afro-American* newspaper: "Mrs King told the seven-thousand-strong audience that her late husband's spirit is with us tonight. He had great affection for you as a people and was greatly inspired by your motto, 'Out of Many, One People'."

Later research showed that the Dr King had also visited Jamaica on 20th June 1965. Accompanied by his wife, he delivered an address at the graduation ceremony at the University of the West Indies, Mona campus, and then spoke to the public at the national stadium. He was, apparently, profoundly affected by his short sojourn in Jamaica.

Martin Luther King, Jr believed that the freedom he was fighting for in the US was to be seen in action in Jamaica, a politically independent, majority Black nation. He felt so comfortable in Jamaica that he returned again in February 1967 and rented a house in Ocho Rios where he completed the manuscript which became his most important book, *Where Do We Go From Here?*

It appears that he chose Jamaica to write in not only because it provided an opportunity to reflect without distractions, but also because his spirit and vision were inspired by this independent, Black nation.

BOB MARLEY, THE WAILERS, PELÉ, AND ALLAN COLE

One of my friends, Winston Carty, was a very talented footballer who went on to play for Jamaica's under-19 team, but our real idol at the time was Allan 'Skill' Cole. Allan was a good friend of reggae legend, Bob Marley, and was also Marley's road manager on several tours with The Wailers. On quite a few occasions we would pick out an area to play on and then Allan and another player named Leonard (Chicken) Mason would come along and move us to a rougher part of the ground. Since they were older and both played for Jamaica we would move on without protest.

When we later moved to Berkley Avenue in Kingston, Allan was living on Fourth Avenue which was just across the road, and we often saw him and some of The Wailers practising in the back yard. I honestly can't remember noticing Bob Marley because he was just another reggae singer at that time, and there were many of those around Kingston. However, my brother Garnet told me that one day The Wailers were passing by our house to meet up with Allan, and Bob Marley stopped and asked him for an East Indian mango. Garnet gave him a mango, for which Marley thanked him. I subsequently met Allan several times in Vineyard Town, near the shops opposite the Post Office.

However, I never mentioned why he and his friend used to move us down the pitch!

One of the highlights of my years in Jamaica was seeing the great football legend, Pelé at the National Stadium in 1971. Pelé was playing for his club Santos of Brazil, but I only really remember him and another player called Edu. However, what was remarkable about this match was that everything that Pelé did on the pitch, Allan matched him ball for ball. That is the reason Allan's nickname was to become 'Skill' Cole.

I left Jamaica later that year but I was subsequently told by some of my friends that he went to play for Nautica FC in Brazil.

In September 2010, I noted in an article in Jamaica's *Gleaner* newspaper that a beaming Allan 'Skill' Cole was presented with a plaque by FIFA President Sepp Blatter, in recognition of his contribution to Jamaican football. For the 60-year-old former Santos and Jamaica star, the occasion was, apparently, bittersweet. "I really appreciate the award but I think the contribution I could make at a national level is being ignored," Cole told *The Gleaner*. "Apparently, there are people here who don't want to see people like me in a certain capacity."

CHAPTER TWO

Luton, England

I was almost eighteen when I left Jamaica for the UK. I was reading a lot at the time and a friend of mine had a brother living in Brooklyn, New York. My grandmother on my father's side was also living in Brooklyn. My friend Patrick and I often used to talk about the civil rights movement, and the way Black people were treated unfairly. My friends and I did not fully understand it at the time, but we did know that it was wrong. We used to see magazines from the USA, and in one of them I saw a Black man on the pavement being kicked by several white men. This image has remained with me to this day. I also read about Enoch Powell's 'Rivers of Blood' speech in 1968, so wrote to my mother and told her that I did not want to come to England. I therefore developed from an early age a sense of what was right and wrong.

Despite by protests, my parents still sent for us to live with them in the UK. I had been told that my father owned several properties in Luton, but when my brother Garnet and I arrived at the end of March 1971 we discovered that he owned just one house and was not the property tycoon we had perhaps hoped for.

We also had an uncle named Noel Simpson who lived in Spalding, Manchester. Our mother used to send myself and my brothers to stay with him during the summer holidays. Uncle Noel was a supervisor and chef at Cobbla Camp which was a residential home for boys. He had a son named Charlie who was about my age. We spent most of the time running around the camp playing cricket, and only going to see our uncle at lunch-time for our meal. One weekend we went to watch a cricket match at the camp and I saw a young man named Johnny make a century. The batting was brilliant, but what amazed me was the fact that he did not wear a pair of batting gloves against some fast bowlers. He was the talk of the area for several months.

FAMILY

I met my wife Pamela by accident during the Easter of 1972. I was going to a dance at the Corn Exchange in Bedford where I had arranged to see a young lady named Jacqui Wilson. Jacqui and I had met before at another dance at the West Indian Club and we had agreed to meet at the Corn Exchange. I duly arrived there with my friend Franklin Hunter, but after waiting some time for Jacqui it looked as if she was not coming. I then saw this beautiful woman with a large Afro, a hairstyle that was very fashionable at the time. I said to Franklin that the young lady looks like someone from Luton College of Higher Education where I was studying part-time. I approached her and she told me that she was not from Luton, but from Erdington in Birmingham. She was training as a nurse and had come to Bedford with a friend who was already a nurse. Her friend's partner was playing in the visiting band. Pamela was very shy at first, and refused to come outside with me. However, eventually she did, and I was able to persuade her to give me her address and phone number. In those days there were no mobile phones, so we wrote to each other before I was finally invited to visit her family in Birmingham. Fortunately, I was immediately made welcome by Mr Ruel Griffiths, Pamela's step-father, and her mother Myrtle Griffiths.

On our dates we went to various night clubs in Birmingham such as the Ridgeway and Rialto. Luton did not have any clubs of this type, and I felt very much at home in Handsworth which reminded me of Jamaica. In those

Our wedding day. Pamela and I were
married in Luton on 2 August 1975.

days we were always overjoyed when we walked into a club
that was full of Black Caribbean people like ourselves.

During this period I became good friends with Hopeton
Miller who lived with his family on the same road as Pamela.
Hopeton had a car, and we went everywhere together for
several years. Eventually, Pamela moved to Luton, and we
were married on 2nd August 1975.

Pamela and I have been happily married now for more
than 46 years and are blessed with two daughters – Andrea
and Simone. My working life has undergone many changes
from those early days at Chrysler and I have certainly
witnessed many things as a social worker, including abject
poverty and the suffering of my fellow human beings.
Nevertheless, I have always tried to show my humanity to
people regardless of race, class, gender or social standing.
However, nothing could have prepared either myself or my
family for what happened to our youngest daughter Simone
in August 2016, as out of the blue she was diagnosed with
breast cancer.

The day she was given the news Simone came out of
the hospital and we all went to her sister Andrea's house. I
recall that I was sitting with Simone alone whilst Pamela

and Andrea went to the shops. Simone turned to me in tears and said, "Dad, why me, why me? All my life I have not done harm to anyone". I, in turn, was stumped for words for perhaps the first time in my life. I can't even remember what I uttered to comfort our distraught daughter, but I do know that I tried to remain positive.

Immediately after being told about her illness, two of our friends started to pray for Simone's recovery. One of these was Jimmy Adams, a former captain of the West Indies cricket team who is a devout Christian and was both a coach and a member of the prayer group in Kent. The other was Sharon, a social work colleague from Trinidad who was in my team in Swindon. Sharon also explained to me about the different stages of cancer, and told me that that one of her relatives had stage four, whilst I told her that Simone was at stage three.

Many friends contacted us and offered lots of support, as well as people we were less acquainted with. Several former and current West Indies cricketers contacted Simone on a regular basis to wish her well. Our extended family and friends in England and Jamaica showered Simone with beautiful gifts and prayers which lifted her spirits and for which she was grateful.

With Pamela and our daughters, Andrea and Simone, at the Centennial Centre in Birmingham in 2004.

On holday in 2011 with Pamela at the Royal Dragon Hotel in Turkey.

I also received excellent support from my senior manager Debbie Curd and my line manager Jo. I was given permission to leave the office at any time to visit Simone. Pamela was also working at that time, and she received lots of help, support and time off to attend Simone's hospital visits with her. Simone received excellent treatment at the Great Western Hospital in Swindon for which we, as a family, are truly grateful.

I cannot thank enough all those who supported Simone and our family throughout these difficult years. I cannot name everyone, but I am sure they know who they are.

When Simone started chemotherapy she became very ill and had to stay in bed for days, with her mother Pamela being the main carer. Pamela was beside herself with grief and would often be in tears during these times.

The lowest point in my life was when Simone went to have surgery. I sat in the waiting room looking lost whilst Pamela followed Simone to the door of the operating theatre and came back with tears in her eyes. We then went home and kept praying that she would wake up from the operation. We have heard people say many times that a child should not die before their parents, and Pamela and I certainly had this terrible thought on our minds. After waiting for what felt like an eternity we finally received a call from the hospital that she was out of surgery and we both breathed a huge sigh of relief. Simone told me later that she always remembered that look on my face when she was in the hospital.

I am so pleased to say that God listened to ours and our friends' prayers, and although Simone is still having treatment she is now making good progress. Despite everything, she has remained brave throughout and has stayed positive whilst having to endure so many different drugs and treatments. Just recently, Simone heard the good news that after three years of study during her cancer treatment, she has passed her Sports Coaching Course with distinction.

My sisters Beverlyn, left, and Arlene.

At a dinner and dance in 1998 with my mother and brothers. Back row from left: Harvey, Mark and Garnet; front row: Fred, our mother, Pearl, and me.

CHRYSLER

I began playing cricket in1972 when I got a job at Chrysler, a truck production plant in Dunstable, Bedfordshire. There were only three Black men working in this factory then, and one of them was a talented cricket all-rounder named Norman Levy. We quickly became good friends and he gave me some good advice on how best to survive in England.

Norman noticed that I was very generous and always bought rounds of drinks after cricket matches. He also observed that some people in the factory liked borrowing money. He told me that people would take my kindness for weakness, and that I should not be too generous with my own money. Later in life, Norman and my other good friend Roy Eubank from St Elizabeth, affectionately known as 'Red' Roy, both encouraged me to buy my council house in Luton. Roy also gave me similar advice about being too kind.

Some while later, another Jamaican, Ossie Clarke, started working at Chrysler, and he turned out to be probably one of the best all round cricketers I ever played with. Ossie came to the factory as a welder and immediately joined the cricket team. I recall one game in particular when he opened the batting and hit the first ball out of the ground for six runs. This was really amazing because we were always told that batsmen, and especially opening batsmen, should watch the first few balls on to the bat. I asked Ossie why he went on the attack so early, and he just said in a flippant manner: "Steve, it was an off volley and it was there to be hit, so I hit it."

Ossie was also a brilliant bowler and fielder of an extremely high standard, and I am certain that if he had remained on the island he could have played first-class cricket for Jamaica. If it had not been for the racism he encountered in England, he would have done well in a County Cricket team if he had only been given the chance.

Ossie told me he had been coached by Dickie Fuller, who was well known in Jamaica. This was apparent when I first saw him playing for Chrysler, and when he later captained Luton United and won all the local competitions. In later years when I watched a lot of county cricket I remained convinced that he was potentially a better player than most of the young men who were given contracts based on their class and family connections, rather than their talent.

Together we played for Chrysler for about three years and once played a West Indian team named Luton United. We were soundly beaten by this team, with only myself and Norman making any runs. I also played a few matches for Caribbean Cavaliers along with Ossie Clarke, and I remember taking four wickets in my first match against Hazelmere cricket club.

THE POWER OF LUTON UNITED

Eventually I was encouraged to join Luton United by several of my friends, so both my brother Garnett and I went on to play for them before he went to live in Birmingham.

Terry Gooding was a talented batsman and local cricket historian and he told me that he joined Luton United in 1974 after the Caribbean Cavaliers folded. Several of their younger players eventually filtered into United, along with myself and Garnett. Terry Gooding wrote the following:

"Luton United became the most feared local cricket team throughout the late seventies and early eighties. They dominated all the local cup competitions but for some reason could not win the Luton News Mid-Week League cup until 1983.

Under the leadership of Ossie Clarke, United batsmen scored runs in abundance in the weekend friendly matches. The bowlers were also in devastating form. Many players left the club through frustration, because they rarely got a chance to bat. The top five batsmen hardly failed."

Luton United Cricket Club at Trent Bridge in 1977 during the Ross Pub National 7-a-side Competition. Back Row (l-r): E. Abraham, H. Manning, S. Stephenson, O. Clarke, T. Prescott; front row: G. Michael, T. Gooding, U. Burgess. Photo courtesy Calvin Terry Gooding

On the few occasions that the tail-enders were called on to bat they always seized the opportunity by putting on good partnerships to either draw or win the game. I am so pleased that Terry mentioned this because I was one of those players along with Raymond Lormond and David Burris, known affectionately as Trini. United batting was so strong that we would often make over 200 runs and lose only 3 or 4 wickets.

My Chrysler friend Ossie Clarke was an outstanding all-rounder and skipper. Whenever United looked to be struggling he would always produce the runs or wickets to get the team back on track.

The nucleus of players for United at that time was: Noel Abbey, Andrew Antrobus, Utel Burgess, David Burris ('Trini'), Raymond Lormond, Harry Lloyd, Elliston Abraham, Dipak Parsooth, Ossie Clarke, Gerrard Michael, Trevor Prescott, Garnet Stephenson and myself.

Luton United Cricket Club. I am pictured standing far left with what were the new generation of players in 1982. Photo courtesy Calvin Terry Gooding

Luton United Cricket Club played a significant role in the development of West Indian club cricket in the area. Brilliantly led by Ossie Clarke, United became one of the most respected and successful clubs in Bedfordshire, on and off the field. In 1978, the club made a historic tour to East Berlin, Germany, returning with a result of six unbeaten matches. A Trinidadian soldier named Tony Ali who was in the second battalion of the Royal Anglian regiment based in Kent had invited United to Germany as he was a friend of our captain Ossie Clarke.

The other prominent cricket club which became United's main rival was Chevette CC which was formed in 1975. Many of their players worked at Vauxhall Motors in Luton, and were employed on the line that built the Chevette car, hence the club's name.

Luton United folded in the late 1980s due to a lack of quality players. They tried their best to keep things going but, in the end, all that remains are great memories of the most feared club in local cricket.

HENRY RHINEY

Apart from great cricketers, I also worked with Henry Rhiney at Chrysler in the days before the word 'celebrity' became so fashionable. He and I used to sit together every lunch break. Although he was a top class boxer he was also a quiet, likeable, and pleasant individual and a good footballer who played for Ebony Starlight Football Club before I became chairman. I remember another good player and friend, Donald Hamilton, telling me that Henry had the record of scoring ten goals for Ebony in one match.

Henry Rhiney made his professional boxing debut in April 1973. He won most of his early fights, but was beaten twice in 1974 by Pat Thomas. He won his first professional title in October 1976, stopping Mickey Ryce in the eighth round to become southern area welterweight champion. Two months later he fought Thomas again for the latter's British title, avenging the earlier defeats with an eighth round stoppage to become British champion.

In December 1978, he challenged for Josef Pachler's European welterweight title in Dornbirn, Austria. Henry stopped Pachler in the tenth round to add the European title to his British belt. This was a very proud moment for me personally and also for the people of Luton, especially the Black Caribbean community.

He made a defence of the European title in January 1979 against Dave 'Boy' Green at the Royal Albert Hall, losing after Green stopped him in the fifth round. Although Henry lost the title we were all still proud of him. I remember that fight well because it was my first trip to a boxing match at the Royal Albert Hall. The Ebony football players clubbed together and we took two full coaches of supporters to watch his match.

In April 1979, he made a second defence of his British title against Kirkland Laing who stopped him in the tenth round. Henry subsequently relocated to Florida.

CHAPTER THREE

Sporting Matters

As I mentioned earlier, Luton United had folded towards the end of the 1980s, and a few years later both Chevette and Luton International decided that it would be best to combine their resources into one club. As Terry Gooding comments: "Black cricket had been on a downward slide for years. Both clubs were unable to attract any new players and unlike the Asian players, cricket was not in the blood of the British born young West Indians." An amalgamation therefore made sense as it would extend the long term future of West Indian club cricket in Luton.

The wheels were set in motion in February 1994 and the proposed name for the club was Luton Caribbean Cricket Club (LCCC). The rules and constitution were duly drawn up and the foundations were put in place to hopefully take Black-led cricket to another level.

I was the president of the new club and the vice president was Ossie Lewis. The founders were: Hyden Andrews, Godfrey Arthur, Dudley Belone, Veronica J Joseph, Elwood Smith and Alex St Ville.

The following were made life members: Godfrey Arthur, Veronica J Joseph, Elwood Smith, Patricia Smith, Leslie Joseph, Neville Burke, Winston Service, G Campbell, Lloyd Patterson, G Gonzales and Roy Wilkinson.

Terry Gooding was appointed first team club captain, and the playing members in 1994 were Andrew Antrobus, Noel Abbey, Elliston Abraham, Hayden Andrews, Eddie

Burrows, Cleo Burrows, Raphael Bernard, Gabriel Bernard, Dudley Belone, Donavan Bascombe, Dalton Browne, Ken Davis, Godfrey Davis, Terry Gooding, Neville James, Steve Harewood, Lynden Johnson, Alford Jackson, Ossie Jackson, Ricky Justin, Vincent Justin, Les Jackson, Robbie Lyle, Laurie Lyle, Ossie Lewis, Kenroy Mingo, Leroy Morris, Horace Manning, Trevor Prescott, Aubyn Strachan, Cleve Strachan, Alex St Ville, Lewin Winter, Ronny Woodley, Howard Wedderburn and Cylus Charles.

GERALDINE BURTON

In his book, *They Gave the Crowd Plenty Fun* (Hansib, 2020), Colin Babb referred to my contribution to West Indian club cricket in Britain by outlining my long-established support for the game. "In 1992, Steve Stephenson helped to create the Victoria Mutual Caribbean Cup. Steve Stephenson was the chairman and Courtney Walsh the competition honorary president. The VM Cup was a national competition for West Indian cricket and social clubs in Britain."

I would hasten to add that Dr Beverly Lindsay a successful businesswoman and positive role model who started the VM competition with the support of Francis Nation. It was called the Jamaica Cup but since it was a Caribbean competition I changed the name to one which I felt was more appropriate. Dr Lindsay continued to support cricket and other community events as chair of the Association Jamaica Nationals in Birmingham.

I am one among many to have helped develop West Indian cricket clubs in Britain and there are some outstanding individuals and characters that helped in this endeavour. My friend, the highly respected Geraldine Burton, who has relocated to Jamaica, is one such person. Geraldine was the former chairperson of Luton Caribbean Cricket Club (LCCC); one of the best run clubs that played in the VM Cup. Along with the support of her husband Claude Burton she supported the four events that the VM Cup Committee held on an annual basis: The final, the dinner, public draw and Winston Davis annual benefit match. She has also been a loyal supporter of the West Indies cricket team for almost sixty years, and sat on the committee of the Bedfordshire mid-week cricket league. During this period she mentored and helped young players and said, "We had some success with the youngsters and some went on to play for Bedfordshire County Cricket Club."

In addition, Geraldine performed other roles at LCCC as the club's official scorer and fixture secretary and she could be seen at many weekend matches also helping to make the tea as well as serving. During the interval, if any players were underperforming, she would also engage in impromptu pep talks to spur on the players.

Geraldine was given a special award by the VM Cup Committee for services to cricket alongside her able and competent secretary Veronica Joseph. Geraldine has continued to be a passionate supporter of cricket in Jamaica and in her own words, "I can be seen often on the terraces still being vociferous in supporting local and international matches."

Although cricket has often been seen as a man's game, LCCC and the cricket fraternity in Britain owe her a great debt of gratitude. Her presence is greatly missed in Luton and amongst the fans of the clubs that she used to visit.

FRANKLIN HUNTER

Franklin Hunter was an ardent supporter of Luton United and the West Indies cricket team. He took me to my first Test match in England at the Oval in 1973, and I remember we had to leave Luton at about six in the morning to get there.

Franklin was one of the few young Caribbean men to own a car, and he took my brother Garnet and I to many night clubs all over the country. He also took me to Leeds where I first saw snow. Our favourite club was the All Nations in London, and we also went to another called Burtons a few times.

Franklin went on to play his part in the development of West Indian club cricket, both locally and nationally. During the early days of Ossie Clarke and Luton United, Franklin, Ossie Lewis and I, along with others, felt that Luton United should have joined the Clive Lloyd Cup and tested our skills on the national stage. However, we were still conquering Luton and Bedfordshire at that time. In fact, United became the first Caribbean team to win the coveted Oliver Shield in 1976.

Franklin always felt that Luton had talented cricketers who could compete against any club in the country, so he decided to form a Luton Combined team. This team went on to play firstly in the Clive Lloyd competition and later in the Victoria Mutual Cricket Cup competition. I have fond memories of this because the first match was against Railton Road CC in Brixton. My friend, and one of my favourite cricketers Elliston Abrahams, was late for the match. Franklin told me that I was the best fielder around, so I got the opportunity to play as a substitute in the first ever Clive Lloyd match. As an ordinary club cricketer who could not make the first eleven team, this was a great honour for me to run out with some of the best cricketers in Luton.

At that time, clubs like Caribbean Commonwealth, Starlight CC and Bristol West Indian CC were three of the top teams in the country. However, Luton Combined beat the great Bristol West Indian team and won the coveted Clive Lloyd Cup in 1995, when my friend Ossie Lewis was manager. Ossie felt that the team needed to apply themselves and get the basics right in order to win. This was borne out when Arun Patel and Ken Davis opened the batting for Luton against two excellent fast bowlers in the form of Trevor Samuels, a former West Indies under-19 cricketer, and Kirk Hamilton a former Jamaica under-19 cricketer. Ken and Arun saw off the onslaught of brilliant swing bowling to give United a solid start. Arun scored 70 runs and Donavon Bascombe scored a further 65 runs to take Luton to victory.

Franklin has now successfully relocated to Jamaica where he continues to enjoy cricket along with Elleston Abrahams and other friends from Luton.

KENROY MINGO

One of the cricketers with whom I formed a close bond was Kenroy Mingo from St Vincent who was also a member of the Starlight Youth Club cricket team.

One of the things I remain sad about is being unable to attend Kenroy's funeral in Luton. I had a reception for the full West Indies team in Bristol on that same day, but was unable to get transport to take me to Luton for the funeral. I was unable to drive due to complications from recent foot surgery.

However, I did meet up with Kenroy in Campbell Park, Milton Keynes in 2017 at the Lashings World XI match and we hugged and took photos with each other. I think it was fitting that the last place I saw Kenroy was at a cricket match. Without any doubt he was one of the most talented batsmen of his generation, and is still greatly missed by all in Luton. The problems following the surgery also caused me to miss the funeral of my other great friend, footballer Cyrille Regis in January 2018.

With Kenroy Mingo in 2017 at the cricket match between Lashings CC and the Friends of the Caribbean in Milton Keynes

TONY LESLIE

I cannot mention cricket in England or West Indies cricket without mentioning Tony Leslie.

On 29 March 2021, my brother Garnet phoned to remind me that both of us have been in the UK for fifty years. Over the past half a century I have met some amazing people, but no one more so than Tony Leslie (affectionately known as T Leslie) who, like me, was a social worker by profession. He was a gifted after-dinner speaker and master of ceremonies at many events in our community. He was a regular MC at the Victoria Mutual Caribbean Cup annual dinner and dance as well as our annual cricket draws. He was also an MC at the ground breaking annual Commonwealth Sports Awards founded by Al Hamilton.

In addition, Tony took to the microphone at most of our cricket finals when we presented the trophies to the winners. Tony was supported at many of these events by Murna Eubanks who was also an MC at the VM presentation and dinner in Bedford in 2006. Like Tony, Murna was a pleasant and likeable individual who supported most of my events.

I first saw Tony at the Commonwealth Sports Awards on a few occasions, but did not get to know him until we both went on a three-week cricket tour to Jamaica, organised by Lafrance Gordon from Bristol West Indian Cricket Club. In Jamaica, Lafrance was struggling with all the administration and arrangements so he asked me and Tony to assist him in managing the team. I became manager, with Tony as deputy.

Several hilarious moments took place during the tour that we still laugh about now. One of these moments was when Lafrance decided to look for a friend in Trench Town, West Kingston. A few people told us that it was not safe to do so, but Tony said he was not scared of anyone. I also told the group that I was born in Kingston and knew the area. We went into a bar and Tony ordered white rum and started talking about cricket and a group of local young men gathered around on hearing his strong Jamaican accent.

Whilst we were there several team members kept saying that we needed to leave before it got dark. Tony then jokingly said that he was in charge and was not leaving until he drank enough rum because he was the 'baddest' man in the area. Eventually, one of the young men went away and came back to inform us that the 'Don' in the area gave us permission to stay as long as we wanted. Tony was very pleased to hear this, and kept repeating that he was definitely now the 'baddest' man in Jamaica. We were eventually escorted out of the area by one of the young men. Tony spent the rest of the tour telling everyone how he had conquered West Kingston!

There was another event I particularly recall before the West Indies played England in Bristol in 2009. Tony called me at the last minute saying he was coming to our home to stay and wanted tickets for the match. I told him it was too late as all the tickets had gone, but he would not take 'no' for an answer and said he was still coming to Bristol. I phoned Chris Gayle to tell him that there was a bald-head man who was claiming to be the West Indies number one supporter and demanding a ticket for the game. Chris laughed and went to the manager and obtained another ticket.

One of the saddest days for my wife and I happened in January 2010 when we received a call informing us that Tony had passed away. He had worked hard all his life. During a visit to our home just a year before his death, he spoke about really looking forward to his retirement and spending his days watching cricket mainly at the Oval and Lords. Tony died at the age of 65, before he received his pension, and did not realise his dream.

I gave a speech at Tony's funeral in London in the presence of about six hundred people, and there was a lot of laughter which I knew the great man would have appreciated. Below is an extract from the speech:

"How best can we describe the Great Man? 'T. Les' was a larger than life character. Firstly, he was bald, bold, brash and brave, and I will give you an example: During the 2005 cricket tour of Jamaica, we played a game at Kensington and Tony was captain of the team and I was manager. We won the toss and Tony elected to bat. We gave the umpire the batting line up and the players begun to warm up. All of a sudden Darren Powell, the West Indies fast bowler, walked through the gates of the Kensington Oval. John Hansen, Dennis Chambers and Denzel Owen ('Dreadie') were some of the players in the team. Three talented cricketers, but all of sudden no one wanted to open the batting; number one and two batsmen wanted to go 11; number 3 and 4 batsmen wanted to go 9, 10, Jack.

John Hansen said he is going at No. 6, Dennis Chambers said he wanted to go at No. 7, no one was left to open the batting. After calling several people various names that can't be repeated in this church, Tony decides to open the batting and face the first ball from Darren Powell.

'T. Les' only lasts one over, but that was the essence of the man. Despite the fact that John and Dennis saved the innings, Tony went around the island telling everyone that all the cricketers ran from Powell, who was bowling over 100 mph and he was the only one who stood against him. By the time we left the island it was 200 mph that Powell had bowled to Tony!"

At the end of the speech I made an announcement that for the annual Winston Davis Match in Bristol that year, Winston and I had agreed that the two teams who are usually captained by two former Test players will play for the Tony Leslie Cup. Louise, his partner, duly attended the match in Bristol which helped to make it special. I still have not come to terms with Tony's passing.

The former England cricketer, Michael Carberry made the following heart-warming tribute to T. Les:

"Thank you for all your love and support over the years. You never lost faith in me when others did and that epitomises the man you are. Words right now can't begin to describe how much I will miss you, your humour, your addictive personality and the famous laugh but I know you are in a better place pardner, at peace and will continue to look over me. Sleep peacefully pardner."

Michael summed up what Tony's and my cricket philosophy stands for. We have loyally supported and mentored club, first-class and Test cricketers over the years. This is the reason we have gained the confidence and trust of so many. I have continued to support and advise Michael and I am sure that Tony would have fully appreciated this.

RACISM IN CRICKET

The Victoria Mutual Caribbean Cup and Clive Lloyd Cup Competitions were brimming with Black and Asian cricketers who played second XI county cricket and never made it to the first teams, despite their immense talent.

When I was Chair at the VM Caribbean Cup and also when I was Manager of Birmingham Cavaliers, many cricketers from both the UK and overseas would complain to me about racism and racist attitudes. However, they chose not to take matters further. The overseas players from the Caribbean feared that they would not receive another contract, and the local cricketers feared that it would stop them from progressing to first-class cricket.

In June 2020, I listened to Ollie Robinson's apology on television following his historical racist and sexist tweet during the first Test against New Zealand. I did not see the tweets, so I initially thought that he was probably eighteen years old, and that with race and equality training provided for this cricketer, we could move on. However, Michael Carberry, former England batsman, stated that cricket needed to "weed out" people like Robinson. Carberry, who had twenty years of experience in the game, added that there were people like Ollie Robinson in county cricket, which is really sad to hear about a game that I have followed since I was six years old. Culture Secretary Olive Dowden and Prime Minister Boris Johnson both claimed that the England and Wales Cricket Board (ECB) went over the top by suspending Robinson. But Carberry disagreed with both of them.

I would also add that class has played a big part in hindering the progression of Black players. For example, a lot of minor counties matches were played in mid-week and cricketers who were in a professional job such as a teacher or solicitor could easily take time off in lieu to play. However, a disproportionately high number of Black cricketers worked in factories, and if they took two days off to play a match it would definitely have been without pay.

ACE PROGRAMME

I would like to make a special mention about my friend Ebony Rainford-Brent, MBE, the former England Cricketer, World Cup Winner, Broadcaster, Surrey County Cricket Club Board member and the first Black woman to play cricket for England. Ebony set up the ACE Programme which was launched by Surrey County Cricket Club in January 2020, in response to the decline by 75 per cent in Black British professional players, and who now accounted for less than one per cent of the recreational game overall. The ACE Programme was designed to engage young people of African and Caribbean heritage to take part in the game, and a talent search was launched.

ACE's strategic aim was summed up by a new strapline: 'Supporting Diverse Talent from the Grassroots to the Elite' and the charity's aim was to build grassroots programmes, talent pathways and better talent ID within Black communities; provide elite academy programmes and scholarships to talented players, allowing them to fulfil their potential; and develop a diverse coaching and volunteer scheme through targeted training and mentoring programmes.

As well as Rainford-Brent, the ACE Programme Charity will be championed and supported by four newly appointed Honorary Patrons: former West Indies fast bowler and now Sky Sports commentator Michael Holding; veteran journalist and broadcaster Sir Trevor McDonald; the first Black cricketer to play for England, Roland Butcher, and Olympic gold medallist Denise Lewis.

Sport England provided funding of £540,000 to be delivered over a three-year period, which will enable the programme to employ four full time staff and to create opportunities for far greater numbers of young people. It will be chaired by Ebony Rainford-Brent,

In addition to the Sport England funding, the ACE Programme has also received a grant from the ECB, allowing a programme to be launched in Birmingham. This will be delivered in association with Warwickshire County Cricket Club and be overseen by ACE's first Director of Programmes, Chevy Green – who becomes ACE's first full time employee.

Chevy's sports development experience has seen him progress from a community coach, to development officer to participation manager, which has provided him with the knowledge, experience and passion to lead the ACE Programme as Director.

I was pleased to be invited as a positive role model to the launch in Handsworth, Birmingham, which was headed by Eaton Gordon who was a member of the VM Caribbean Cup National Committee. I met Chevy at this event, and was impressed with what I heard from this young man.

I am very happy to note that two talented cricketers in the form of Dylan Young and Renal Stewart from Bristol have been selected after trials, and also Troy Henry from St Albans West Indies Cricket club whom I personally recommended for a place on the programme.

When I was chair of the VM Caribbean Cup we had started an under-17 national competition, but were only able to run for two years due to lack of funding. Hopefully, ACE will be able to support their players for a much longer period of time. The VM Cup is also proud of the fact that we gave a Special Award to Rainford-Brent in 2007, for Services to Cricket.

EBONY STARLIGHT FOOTBALL CLUB

The year 2022 will mark the 50th Anniversary of the Ebony Starlight Football Club, which was formed in 1972 by a group of young men born in the Caribbean. The original concept of an all-Black team was hatched in 1971, when two of the founder members, Carlos Gordon and George Esnard, created West Indian Wanderers, which then became an affiliated club with the Bedfordshire Football Association under the name of Ebony FC.

The following individuals are recognised as being the founders as they were all part of the club during its transition from a friendly team to its first full season of organised football, namely, Abraham Aarons, Peter Atkinson, Tom Brock (the only non-Caribbean and non-Black player,) Evans Clarke, Ossie Clarke, Henry Charlton, Steve Clouden, Leslie Scafe, George Esnard, Carlos Gordon, Eth Gustave, Donald Hamilton, Clubert Hendrickson, Noel Lewis, Richard Lockheed, Tony McDermott, Launder Philogene, Henry Rhiney, Clayton Thomas, Vincent Williams and Roy Young.

Ebony Starlight Football Club in 1978. I am pictured standing third from left with my brother, Harvey, fourth from left. Photo courtesy Noel Lewis

Ebony Starlight FC at Caesar's Palace in Luton featured
in *Luton News* in 1978. Photo courtesy Noel Lewis

In the early days, the players used to meet at a small
club affectionately known as 'Donkey Pen', they also used
the Starlight Youth Club in the mornings for a while. When
I joined Ebony in 1974, Vince Williams was the manager,
Noel Lewis was Secretary and other Committee members
were James Philip, Dicky Williams, Earl Thomas, Van
Clarke and Ricky Thomas.

Noel Lewis our player/secretary played a big part in
getting Ricky Hill interested in Ebony FC. Ricky became
the fourth Black player to play for England, yet he was a
very modest individual. However, once he knew of our
existence, Ricky took an immediate interest and helped train
the team as well as giving advice.

The nucleus of the first team during my time with the
club was Noel Lewis, Carlos Gordon, James Philip, Van
Clarke, Steve Clouden, Albert Hunter, Dougal Martin, Derek
Phipps, Dean Blackett, Valbert Foster, Peter Thompson,

Percy Wallace and Patrick Markland. Richie Richardson, who became a professional footballer in Holland, joined the club later along with Godfrey Arthur, George Celine, Venol King, Albert Hunter, Donald Hamilton, Tony Lettman, Desmond McPherson, Ezra Simon, Tony Sterling, Harvey Stephenson and others from the local community.

The period when I became involved with football coincided with a lot of racial harassment from the police towards young Black people. Noel Lewis, who we used to call 'Mr Ebony', was also a talented footballer. He was the best reader of a football match I ever met, even after I became involved with Cyrille Regis and met many other professional footballers.

Noel asked me to become chairman of Ebony FC during the period that I was leader of the Starlight Youth Club, and thus able to give the players the use of the building to meet in on Sunday mornings before matches. We had a first and second team so we often had about sixty people in the building which included players and supporters.

After matches we would all meet in the Dutchman Pub in Bury Park for a drink and lots of banter. The atmosphere was brilliant and I enjoyed meeting the players and their supporters after the games. It was even better when both teams won, and also if the Saturday team did. I had several young players from the youth club in the Ebony FC second team, and I was always keen to hear about their performances. Patrick Markland and Danny Nugent were two talented players who were always at the youth club and my brother Harvey, a belligerent striker, was also in Ebony's second team. Some of our best players played good standard non-league football and were potentially good enough for the old third and fourth divisions in the English Football League.

I completed the sponge man/first aid course under John Moore, who later became Luton Town's manager. It is interesting to note that my first Test as a sponge man came the same week of finishing the course. Ebony was playing at Kingsway Park when the goalkeeper in another match broke his leg, and the team did not have a first aider in attendance. I helped put his legs together for support and wrapped them whilst waiting for the ambulance. Afterwards, all the players from his team expressed their gratitude for my help.

Later, I wrote to John and recommended two players for trial with Luton Town FC. John did not reveal when someone would be sent to observe the players in action. He later reported to me that one was talented, but did not do much when he was not in possession of the ball and felt he had the wrong attitude.

There was still a lot of racism and stereotypes about Black players then, with ideas that they did not like the cold and a belief that they had weak ankles. However, a steady stream of Black players came to play for Luton and began to change that ill-conceived negativity and perception. As far as I was concerned, Ricky Hill was the first and most influential player who got involved with Luton. Ricky was really the first celebrity that I knew as a friend, yet he was so humble and modest.

Other Black footballers also began to play for Luton Town such as Mitchell Thomas, Brian Stein, Mark Stein and Paul Elliott. We were especially proud of Mitchell who played for Limbury FC as a youth player, whilst some of his brothers played for Ebony FC. Mitchell was on the YTS (Youth Training Scheme) and eventually went on to play for Luton Town, Tottenham Hotspur and West Ham United. Our pride in Mitchell was because he was Luton born and bred, and also for his connection with the Starlight Youth Club. Although I did not see him often, he knew that people like me were always there for him and were always supporting him.

There was a period when some people used to question me and some of the players about why we had a Black football club, and as the chairman I thought that this was offensive and insensitive. My contention was that there was a Sacred Heart FC which was Catholic, and Celtic

Supporters FC which was Scottish, but no one questioned their right to their own identity.

We had a similar situation with our West Indian cricket club, but maybe less so because the team was named Luton United CC which appeared to be more acceptable than the Black name of Ebony FC.

Ebony had been formed because of the same reasons that Black churches developed in the UK. This was as a result of racist attitudes and rejection by the mainstream churches. There were numerous stories circulating about individuals from Christian denominations in the Caribbean that arrived in the UK with letters from English clergy in their respective islands, only to be turned away by the local church. My friend, Enrico Stennett, told me how he had arrived in Britain in 1947 before the momentous arrival of the *Empire Windrush* in 1948. He started attending the Warwick Road church in London with two friends. On the second Sunday the priest met them at the door and told Enrico and his friends that they were no longer welcome because they were upsetting the regular members.

The Ebony footballers had similar experiences while playing for white clubs. On many occasions they were amongst the star players at their club. However, when presentation evenings came around after winning a division of the league, some had their medals put through their letter box with no invitation to the presentation dinners. Some members of Luton United Cricket Club such as Ossie Clarke shared similar experiences of racism in cricket.

During this period, whenever Black players faced racism on the field and from fans on the side-lines they did not get support from the white managers or their fellow players. If they protested too much they would be dropped from the team and told they had a 'chip on their shoulder'.

Another discriminatory issue that I particularly noticed whilst carrying out the job of sponge man was the definite feeling of us playing against fourteen opponents instead of eleven; the referees and the two linesmen (when appointed) would almost always give the decisions to the opposition team, which was obviously white because we were the only Black club in the league. So, neutrality and being unbiased were non-existent. All the match officials would also rather have a drink with the other team. We always tried to gain a two-goal advantage, if possible, because if the game was close it was common for decisions to rule against us.

CYRILLE REGIS

I owe my friend, the late Cyrille Regis, a great debt of gratitude. The majority of my sports and charity work would not have been possible without him. In my youth as a West Bromwich Albion fan, I was intoxicated by his style of football and the many fantastic goals he scored for the team. I remember when I first went to Birmingham Cyrille was given two VIP tickets by the West Indies team to attend a function at Edgbaston cricket club. He took me and I was able to have personal chats with many of the players. Cyrille also took me to see boxer Nigel Benn fight at the Royal Albert Hall, and afterwards we joined footballers Vinnie Jones and Justin Fashanu, and members of the Black pact in the VIP area. He also took me and his son Robert to Wembley Stadium in 2000 when Aston Villa lost 1-0 to Chelsea in the FA Cup Final. This was the last match to be played at the old Wembley Stadium. Before the match Nigel Kennedy, a world renowned violinist and huge Villa supporter, hired the top floor of a hotel near the grounds and we were invited to have champagne and caviar, and to mingle with a lot of celebrities. All these connections helped me to take my sports and charity work to another level.

I recall a memorable moment after the Nigel Benn fight when he was signing autographs. I joined a queue with twelve people before me, and when I got to the front Nigel looked up at me and signed the photo to my daughter Andrea. I handed him a five pound note which he folded, put back in my hand and uttered the word 'Respect'.

Daughter, Simone, pictured with footballers Mark
Walters, left, and Cyrille Regis in Birmingham in 1989.

In Cyrille's autobiography, *Cyrille Regis: My Story*, co-
author, Chris Green wrote, "If you're going to have heroes,
have great ones". Generally, heroes turn out to be a
disappointment as they are rarely the people they seem or
what we want them to be. Why should they be? Too often
fans put heroes on unbelievably high pedestals. Cyrille
Regis, however, stands apart and remains my hero. I fully
agree with Chris's statement as he and Ricky Hill were two
of the main footballers that I looked up to when I was Chair
of Ebony FC in Luton.

In his book Cyrille stated:

"The legend of my football career can be condensed
into a few simple facts. I was spotted on Regents Park,
signed by two non-league clubs, first Moseley, then
Hayes, sold to First Division West Bromwich Albion,
scoring on my debut and becoming one of Alboin's all-

At home in Swindon with Ricky Hill, left, and Cyrille Regis in 2005.

time heroes. I was an England centre-forward and FA
Cup-winning medallist with Coventry City and had
late playing career resurgence at Villa and Wolves."

These comments are quite modest as during one of the VM
Caribbean Cup events I told the late Tony Leslie, our beloved
MC, to introduce Cyrille as the doyen of Black British
footballers. Cyrille said he was honoured by the title which
I said was well deserved as it was the title given to the
great Trinidadian cricketer and politician, Lord Learie
Constantine.

DWIGHT YORKE

I met Dwight at Aston Villa in 1989 when Graham Taylor
signed him from Signal Hill FC in Trinidad. I remember when
Gary Thompson's elder brother arranged the trip for Aston
Villa to go to Trinidad. Although we did not become personal
friends, I made an effort to make sure Dwight was okay.

When he arrived in England he was living with Tony
Daley's mother in Newtown, near Handsworth, and I was
working across the road. He told me his brother Clint was a
professional cricketer in the leagues, so I lent him some

cricket tapes to watch on VHS and some tapes of football matches. I also invited him to our house in Sutton Coldfield for dinner.

I then left Sutton in March 1990 to take up a post in Bedford. 'Yorkie' said that when he came back for the following season he called at our home and a neighbour told him that we had moved away. He then moved to Coleshill and was boarding with a nice elderly couple. I met them in the players' lounge once, and phoned Yorkie a few times but he was never in.

One Saturday I arrived at the players' lounge and saw two Black guys there but they did not look like regulars. I offered them a drink and got talking to them and they mentioned being cricketers from Trinidad, named Dave Williams and Brian Lara! Neither of them played for the West Indies at that time. A few years later I bought some Caribbean food for the West Indies team staying at the Grand Hotel in Birmingham, and reminded Brian of the time when we first met and he gave me a big smile. That evening I received a few extra Test match tickets from him.

One day, I was outside the players' lounge and saw Yorkie coming in. He was not looking too happy because he was not in the team. I told him to have a word with Cyrille Regis who was a personal friend of mine. Yorkie surprisingly said no, because he was competing for the same position as Cyrille. I laughed and said, "Yorkie, Cyrille is now a veteran who has nothing to prove to anybody, he has already played for England and he is the best man to advise you". By the time I told this story to Cyrille, he said that Yorkie had already been to see him.

PAUL MCGRATH

I met Paul also at Aston Villa, and he has been one of the most likeable and pleasant footballers that I have known. I remember there was going to be a big match between Villa and Manchester United in December 1990. Mark Walters was not around, so I could not get a ticket for 'love nor money'. This was a massive game and the whole of Birmingham wanted to be there so Paul came up with a brilliant idea. He said that I was always well dressed in a suit and tie so nobody would question whether I had a ticket or not! So, on the day of the match I was let into the players' lounge by the man at the entrance who knew me quite well by then. Paul then took me through the front entrance past the security and the admin staff, straight to the main stands.

When the fans saw Paul they cleared the way for us and we took our seats beside some Villa fans. After the game (1-1) we went back to the players' lounge where we met David Beckham and the rest of the United team, although David was not a big star at this stage.

At the time, Paul was living near to me in Sutton Coldfield and came to visit our home and meet our daughters. One day he asked if I could pick him up to go "out on the town". I met him in a Sutton Coldfield bar along with Tony Daley and some other Villa players. Some of the fans were a bit noisy and started making comments in our direction. Paul then said that we Black guys need to stick together, and a few people looked around in surprise because Paul was identifying himself as Black; his mother was Irish and his father Nigerian.

For many in Ireland Paul McGrath is a living legend. No player in Ireland's history has had so many headlines written in his honour, yet the defender has always remained modest about his ability. He spent the first sixteen years of his life in an orphanage and started his football career in Ireland with Dalkey United AFC before joining St Patrick's Athletic FC. He won the Young Player of the Year award in 1982, and joined Manchester United for a bargain £30,000 the following season.

TRIBUTE TO THE PIONEERS OF BLACK BRITISH FOOTBALL

Despite the racism and lack of support from the main stream media and major sports companies who refused to sponsor the event, I made history in 1998 by putting on the first and only 'Tribute to the Pioneers of Black British football' event. It was staged at the Centennial Centre in Birmingham.

I had decided to honour the Black footballers who had given so much and brought such pride to our community, and approached Cyrille Regis who gave his one hundred per cent support together with Paul Elliott. Olive Robinson, manager of the ACE centre in Northampton, also provided support along with Nicky Taylor and my friend Bob Baker.

However, I really struggled to get sponsorship for this event, and it was only through Brendon Batson with the support of Gordon Taylor of the Professional Footballers Association (PFA) that they were convinced to donate £3,000 and became the main sponsor. The second sponsor was Paulette Simpson, chief representative at National Commercial Bank in Birmingham and now an executive director of the *The Voice* newspaper. I had approached Piara Power, director of *Kick It Out* for help, and whilst he was supportive and attended the event he was not able to offer any financial support.

The planning of the event was, however, marred by the racist attitudes at the time. I wrote to the Football Trust three times, and did not receive a reply. I wrote to two of the biggest brands in football and they wrote back stating that there was no budget for this type of event. I wrote to several big clubs who refused to donate any memorabilia. Fortunately, there was some kindness from people in the sports industry, and I received a signed shirt from Steve Coppell who was at Crystal Palace.

One major national newspaper promised to cover the event, but they pulled out at the last minute. It was only Rodney Hinds from the *The Voice* that attended, and BVTV, a Black television company, that covered it.

Astonishingly, I was criticised by a number of white people for not including white players. But this would have nullified the specific experience of Black players like Cyrille Regis, Paul Elliott, Mark Walters and Ricky Hill whom I knew personally, and was aware of the racism they had

Tribute to the pioneers of Black British football: This was the first ever tribute to Black British footballers and took place on 30 May 1998 at the Centennial Centre in Birmingham. The event was organised by Steve Stephenson and sponsored by the Professional Footballers' Association (PFA) and the National Commercial Bank of Jamaica.
Pictured, left to right, back row: Denton Thomas, Ricky Hill, Clive Wilson, Godfrey Ingram, Brian Stein and Luther Blissett; middle row: Brendon Batson (PFA), Garth Crooks, Steve Makone, Gerald Francis and Tony Whelan; front row: Cyrille Regis, Clyde Best, Steve Stephenson, Bob Hazell and Mark Walters. Photo by Black-Ink

faced. I made it clear that I was only one man with no major support behind me, except Brendon Batson at the PFA, and could not be expected to put on a tribute for the entire football league!

This ground-breaking event was attended by over three hundred people, with a galaxy of celebrities including thirty Black footballers. These included the former England players Garth Crooks, the late Cyrille Regis, Luther Blissett, Ricky Hill, Mark Walters, Brian Stein, Paul Elliott and Bob Hazell. Three Black footballers now living overseas also attended the event – Clyde Best, the former West Ham FC legend, flew in from Bermuda; the late Steve Mokone, who was the first Black professional footballer from South Africa and who played for Coventry City; and Gerry Francis, a former Leeds United player who came from Canada.

The special guest speaker was Barry Fry who was manager of Peterborough United and a football pundit. Another special guest was actor Tom Watt who played the character 'Lofty' in TV soap, *EastEnders*. The MCs were Jackie Harper from ITN News, and presenter Trish Adudu from Channel Five Sports. Al Hamilton, the founder of the Commonwealth Sports Awards and author of *Black Pearls: The A-Z of Black Footballers in the English Game*, was also in attendance.

On the night a special award was given to the Jamaica Football team – nicknamed the Reggae Boyz – for becoming, in 1998, the first Caribbean country to qualify for the FIFA World Cup.

Phil Vasili, the football historian, was a key-note speaker and he made special mention of Black football pioneer Walter Tull who played as an inside forward and half back for Clapton FC, Tottenham Hotspur and then Northampton Town between 1908 and 1914. Arthur Wharton, another pioneer, was also honoured on the night. He played for Preston North End, Rotherham Town and Sheffield United among others between 1887 and 1902. We were also honoured with the presence of his great granddaughter Sheila Leeson who received the award, along with Howard Holmes from 'Football Unites, Racism Divides'.

A special brochure was produced by Frankie Joseph, a young artist from Luton who also designed the special awards which were framed and presented to each player.

Former Tottenham Hotspur player and now football manager, Chris Houghton was unable to attend but sent a hand written letter in which he congratulated me for organising such an event, remarking that it, "should have been done a long time ago".

Ricky Hill was equally poignant and profound, saying: "I think it is extremely compelling and displays the commitment in the face of racial inequalities that you and

With Liverpool FC football player, John Barnes in 1992.

others have endured. Despite this exclusion you have still managed to find a way to uplift many who not for your efforts would not be counted. The piece is inspiring and should be shared for everyone to truly understand the depths of the struggle for equality even in the UK that has been a lived experience for Black and minority ethnic people."

Later that year, I gave evidence on racism in football to the House of Commons Select Committee, headed by David Mellor and in the presence of Lord Herman Ouseley.

CHAPTER FOUR

Starlight Youth Club

In 2001, the Cantle report, commissioned after the race riots in Bradford, Oldham and Burnley, concluded that the depth of polarisation in segregated communities in some towns will lead to further violence and unrest if the cycle isn't broken. Long before this report was published, I had been involved in trying to develop an inclusive society as a youth and community worker, and later as a social worker.

I had been a member of the management committee at the Starlight Youth Club in Luton since 1975, and worked as a volunteer before I became a senior youth and community worker in June 1980. I was also a founder member of the One Foundation Organisation which was one of the first supplementary schools outside London. This school came about because of Bernard Coard's ground breaking report in 1971 which will be discussed elsewhere in this book. My cricketing friend Franklin Hunter was also a founder member.

The club that became known as the Starlight Youth Club was started at Beech Hill School in Bury Park under the leadership of Arthur Warren. Arthur then returned to Jamaica and his role was taken on by Hannibal Kandekore and then Eliza Prophet. I became the fourth youth leader. The assistant youth leaders at Beech Hill were Beryl Morgan and Muriel Jackson. Arthur and Hannibal were both educated and conscious Black individuals who instilled a sense of pride in all the young people attending the club

Starlight Youth Club in Luton, 1983: (L-R) Harry Sterling, Peter
Thompson, Bob Baker, Francis Reid, me and Derek Spalding.

and who took the time to listen to what they were saying. I
personally learnt a lot from these two men.

Hannibal relocated the club to a building on Inkerman
Street which was then called the 61 Club. A member called
Urschel Smith came up with the name 'Starlight' after
Hannibal suggested 'Ashanti' which was rejected. The next
leader, Eliza Prophet, went on to make a great contribution
to the Caribbean carnival by creating costumes and helping
to organise events. Eliza Prophet was assisted by Ashley
Donn, Beresford Thomas, Maxie Hunter and George Esnard,
whilst I was a member of the Youth Club's management
committee.

My brother Garnett and I were already members of
Starlight, when the club was at Beechill, along with my
friends Franklin Hunter, Joseph and Jacob Alexi, Vaughn
Monroe, Lawrence Palmer, Dicky and Syd Williams,
Jennifer Williams, Elliston Abrahams, his then wife
Thelma, Delroy Smith, Chester Morrison and many others.

We played in the local table tennis league, and my
brother Garnett was unbeaten up to the time the club moved
to Inkerman Street.

In 1979, the Starlight Youth Club was closed down due to lack of funding, so I campaigned, lobbied and bombarded Bedfordshire County Council with the support of Harry and Curly Bruce, Hannibal Kandkore, Valerie Taylor and others for it to be re-opened. Our hard work paid off and the re-opening of the club coincided with the starting of my social work training at Hatfield Polytechnic in 1980. A law student named Carl Campbell joined me as assistant youth worker, along with Laverne Donn and Joyce Scafe.

In order to keep the club afloat, I had to put in some of my own money. Carl also lent me some money, and we purchased basic items including table tennis bats and balls. It should also be noted that the first major support we received came from Superintendent Spaulding of Luton Police, who gave us a new pool table. We also bought sweets to sell, but in those early days we gave away more than we sold!

Paulette Rose became the Secretary of the club and gave me a lot of help in the early days, along with Max Edwards who became a probation officer and went on to make a big contribution to West Indian club cricket in Luton. My wife Pamela, who was an excellent Caribbean caterer, started serving lunches in the summer and these became very popular. Other individuals like Bob Baker, Lawrence Palmer, Bernard Abbey and Philip Rose played a major role in the club during later years. Lawrence Palmer went on to make history when he became the first Black person to become an Area Youth Officer in Luton in 1987.

However, due to the continuing lack of financial and other support for the club, before the summer holidays in 1981, I came up with an idea that has become part of youth work folklore in Bedfordshire. One day, I put on a suit and tie and went into the Arndale Centre and knocked on the manager's door. I told him that I could take the 60 to 80 young people out of the centre who had become a big problem by hanging around, largely because they had nowhere else to go. He surprisingly jumped at my idea, and gave me eight-weeks' funding. My initiative was still being talked about at Youth Work seminars and events long after I left the Youth Service!

Thanks to this funding, I was able to take some club members who played youth cricket for Starlight to away matches with Luton United. This meant that on Saturday or Sunday they would be out of the Arndale Centre from about 12.30 pm and would not return to the area until 10.00 pm. It's hard to estimate how effective these trips were, but at least they were not getting into trouble. It also gave me a chance to talk and connect more with them and also for other Black adult males to do likewise.

One day some of the youths from the Starlight had an altercation with the management of the Snooker Hall in Bury Park. They started breaking up the equipment but luckily I was driving past and intervened to defuse the situation. However, the police came along and tried to arrest me! Luckily, Cllr Hand was in the area and he stopped his car and told the police that I was actually the peacemaker, and they left me alone.

I later pioneered community football and cricket as well as other activities with the police as part of my efforts to help improve race relations and community cohesion in Luton after the uprisings in 1981. I was duly given a testimonial from the Chief Constable of Bedfordshire for helping to bring peace back to Luton. Some years later, another local newspaper interviewed me and published the article under the headline, 'Hero of Race Riot Heads Equality Unit'. The uprisings of 1981 were never a race riot, and I had never seen myself as a hero. I was only making a contribution alongside many other individuals who also played their part. I just happened to be the leader of the club during this challenging period, and it should be noted that Bob Baker, Lawrence Palmer and Bernard Abbey all contributed during and after the uprisings.

BERNARD ABBEY

Affectionately known as Natty, Bernard Abbey, was an original member, and the last leader, of the Starlight Youth Club. He began attending the club because his partner, Glenys, worked there cooking Caribbean food as part of her role to help raise funds.

He volunteered his help in those early days and eventually became a paid youth worker. He was a dedicated member of the club and was also the first person to bring Black comedians to Luton and to the Starlight Youth Club.

Bernard reflected upon the origins of the club: "After arriving in England from the Caribbean in the 1960s, we wanted our own space to share and enjoy our culture, particularly the music. We first used one of our school classrooms and later gathered in the assembly hall as the numbers grew. These gatherings took place two or three evenings a week. A few elder members of the community gave their support which led to the establishment of the youth club. It was located at the Anglican church hall in Inkerman Street and was known as the 61 Club before it was renamed Starlight."

Bernard went on the play a major role in the local Caribbean Carnival.

CONFLICT IN OUR COMMUNITY

Whilst the issue of knife crime amongst Black youngsters in London is high on the agenda, there have also been some serious issues around violence in our own community in Luton. I strongly believe if I and other like-minded people in our community had not intervened, there would have been at least one death, and a young person or an adult male would be serving a prison sentence for murder.

The first situation involved two young people from the Starlight. One youngster was sent to prison, and whilst he was incarcerated his so-called friend started an affair with his girlfriend. The word on the street was that the imprisoned youth was threatening to stab his friend on release. I met him on the day of release at the Youth House in Luton, and he was not in a good mood. Luckily, I managed to diffuse the situation and let him keep his 'street cred' by enabling him to tell all his friends that due to the intervention and pleading by Mr Stephenson he had decided not to carry out the stabbing.

On another occasion, I witnessed a fight between two adult males, both over six foot tall, at a pub in Luton town centre. I had to intervene with some members of the Ebony Football Club. We managed to stop the fight before the police were called. I then spent several weeks speaking to one of them and reporting back to the other before they agreed to call a truce.

The third situation was witnessed by Patrick Markland who was a member of the youth club at the time. Two young men had been fighting in a nightclub. Once again, I intervened with others and then spent time over a six-month period speaking to them and also speaking to their partners, who had also tried to diffuse the situation. It finally came to a point where both of them could keep their 'street cred' by telling everyone that they were persuaded by Mr Stephenson and others to make peace.

It should be noted that in all three conflicts there were a minority in our community encouraging them to settle their differences by 'fighting it out' to see who the best was!

LUTON CARNIVAL

The Luton Archive Project states that in 1976 the first Luton Carnival, as we now know it, was held in the town. This had begun as a Victorian Fayre with a procession and was held to celebrate the 100th anniversary of Luton becoming a borough. Over the years the fair element had declined and now the focus was on the carnival procession.

For the first Caribbean carnival in 1981 the Club was given one truck and a generator. There was, however, a lot of resistance from the council and the police about supposed safety issues. The police insisted that we produce at least

12 Stewards on the day so I asked my brother Harvey, Patrick Chambers, Lawrence Palmer and several other fit young men to volunteer to perform this duty. I also suggested that we end the procession at the top of Inkerman Street, so that people could go straight into Starlight Youth Club and into the adjacent car park. This would help to keep the young people off the streets, which was one of the main concerns of the police.

During the first two carnivals Mrs Prophet and myself plus a few volunteers helped to coordinate and design the making of the costumes and helped to decorate the truck. During those early years of the carnival we used to bring groups and sound systems from London to participate. Harry Bruce who was from Trinidad had some good contacts in London, and he helped to bring in the expertise that was lacking in Luton.

When the council and a few local companies finally realised that the event was viable, stalwarts like Norris Bullock, Rita Clarke, Cllr Desai Stewart and Luton Community Relation Council (CRC) came on board. Later, Teddy Adams from Saint Kitts was employed by the CRC and he helped us to gain more credibility.

As the carnival developed Colin Spalding and others at the club took over the costume making and designs. Once, whilst driving through the countryside, I had a call from Colin who was very excited as he kept saying "thank you" and I replied, "For what?" He said that he had just received a large grant for the carnival. Colin explained how he was inspired by my work in Luton and this led him to start making carnival costumes amongst other things. Colin became the band leader and designer for Rampage Carnival Club, and he has travelled and worked all over the world with his artistic designs and gained national recognition for his work.

In 1998, the Luton Carnival acquired international status, and in 1999, Luton's reputation as a carnival town was cemented with the opening of the UK Centre for Carnival Arts.

THE SUS LAW

When I began volunteering at the Starlight Youth Club many of the Black youths were alienated and marginalised so I set up English and maths classes and encouraged them to go back to college. Many of these young people were struggling with their Black identity. So, in response to this, I set up the first Black Resource Library at the youth club, and began to teach Black Studies. I was also responsible for the first set of multi-cultural books to be put in Luton Central Library when Mr Hawkins the chief librarian asked me to take him to Black bookshops in London.

Later on, as part of my four-year social work degree course, I would write a thesis entitled 'Black Youth Unemployment Causes and Effect' which asked the question, "How is it that a group of young people who were born in the UK in the late 1960s come to be at the bottom of the pile of British society?"

In 1981, Jonathan, a white lecturer from Barnfield College, heard about what I had accomplished with Mr Hawkins and asked me to take him to London to buy similar books. As we approached Brixton a police car pulled us over. We were asked to get out of the car and they searched the boot. John was visibly shaken, and I asked the police in a polite manner why they had stopped us. They claimed that we fitted the description of two people who had committed a robbery.

When the police left, John asked me how I had remained so calm. I told him that as a youth leader this is exactly what I teach the young people to do when they are stopped by the police under the SUS law.

At that time in England and Wales the SUS law (an abbreviation of 'suspected person') was a stop-and-search power that permitted a police officer to stop, search and even arrest people if they suspected that they intended to commit an offence. However, this law caused much public concern, especially amongst the Black community who were disproportionately targeted.

SATURDAY DANCES

Much of what I achieved in Luton would not have been possible without the help of Beanie and Daphne Bernard. We were lucky as a family to live on the Runfold Estate in Luton, and discovered that they were living across the road from us as the only other Black family in the area. Years later my sister Arlene moved into a flat on the corner of the same road.

Having re-opened the Starlight Youth Club in June 1980, the council did not want to offer support because they did not approve of the way the club had been run by the previous leader. As a result, I inherited an empty shell of a building. The Area Youth Office was closely monitoring the club, and I was asked to provide a balance sheet of our income and expenditure on a monthly basis. The only way we were going to make quick money to pay the rent was by having regular dances with the local sound systems that were very popular with our community. There were three locally – one was called Gemini that was run by Lawrence Palmer, another was known as Falcon operated by Eric Vaughn, and finally there was Sovereign run by Crucial Robbie who is now a football pundit and anti-racism campaigner. Beanie had good 'street cred' and agreed to collect money from patrons at the door. This was a difficult job, but he did have the respect of the young people who came to the dances. However, despite our best intentions, we noticed that when these local sound systems played at the club, they were not overly popular and we rarely made enough money to cover our expenses.

One of the members, Francis Reid, who became my right hand man, then came up with the idea of inviting Fat Man and Sir Coxsone sound systems to come to us from London. Fat Man was the first to play at the club and for once the place was full. I could not believe it when Beanie came in with the takings of over £400, which meant that after paying Fat Man I was able to go straight to the bank on Monday morning and deposit £100 towards the rent, saving the club from closure. Fat Man was followed by Sir Coxsone who had deejays like Smiley Culture, Duffus Ire, Festus and Blacka Dredd. Once again the club was full to capacity. The late Smiley Culture went on to have chart success with his songs 'Cockney Translation' and 'Police Officer'. I remembered him being one of the first people who came to the kitchen to order dumplings, ackee and salt fish from my wife Pamela, who provided Caribbean food at these events.

Derek Spalding, a Rastafarian who was on the member's committee, kept asking Pamela to make some coconut drops. She agreed to his request on the understanding that she was going to town to do some shopping, and he should watch the drops whilst they were being cooked. However, when she returned the coconut drops were ruined since they did not come out the way Pamela wanted. Derek had not paid enough attention to the task, but this did not stop him and his friends from eating the spoils.

Derek used to challenge the work that was being done at Starlight, but some years later when I was a visiting lecturer at Hatfield, he admitted that he had not understood just how difficult it was to work and study at the same time, and that I had done both whilst also running the youth club. Derek had finally come to realise that the social work course was quite challenging. Even though we had moved to Sutton Coldfield by then, Derek would travel from Luton to seek my advice and support with his studies.

When I became cultural adviser for BBC Radio Bedfordshire I attended a meeting to discuss bringing a Black Caribbean presenter to the station – Syd Burke, who already had a programme in London. I quickly intervened by telling the producers that Luton had a lot of talented deejays who played at my youth club and that they should be considered. I cannot claim to have got the job for DJs Crucial Robbie or Ezekiel Gray ('the Man Ezekiel'), but had I not intervened, someone outside Luton would have become the presenter.

MUHAMMAD ALI AND PAUL STEPHENSON

It is interesting to note that the history of the Starlight Youth Club had a link with the great boxer Mohammed Ali, through a grant from his foundation in London. After the uprisings in Luton in 1981, I helped to bring peace by starting community cricket and football matches together with the local police force. Paul Stephenson, who was running the Mohammed Ali Sports Foundation in London at that time, came to the Starlight Club when I was the leader, and we posed for a photo outside the club with Teddy Adams, a community activist who was then working for Luton Community Relations Council.

Paul was already well known for leading the Bristol bus strike in 1960 and was an anti-apartheid campaigner. He subsequently invited me to London and gave me money to buy football kit for our players. We then played Bedfordshire police and beat them, which gave many of the youngsters who felt harassed by the police a massive moral victory. To rub salt in the wound we also beat the police at a cricket match at their headquarters in Kempton. The great Muhammad Ali would have been proud of these Black youngsters, if he had known of these victories which were very important to our young people and the wider Black community.

BOB BAKER

Bob Baker and I first met at the Starlight Youth Club and went on to become very good friends. He has supported the majority of my voluntary work over the past 35 years. I describe Bob as "a man of action" because if there is something to be done, Bob will do it. I recall that from the outset he promised to come and help me with some of the projects we were trying to set up. I had told him that we had offers all the time, especially when someone wanted to use the club for a wedding or a party, and that they would make promises but never returned or delivered. Bob proved me wrong by coming to see me more than once over a short period of time. He then played a major role in the youth and community development in Luton and he is still currently active. There is a feeling in some quarters that Bob has not been given enough recognition for his work.

In addition to helping with the Starlight, Bob made a major contribution to the One Foundation Saturday School, along with another of my co-founders, Eileen Williams. Eileen was Secretary of the National Federation of Self Help Organisations, working for Dr Vince Hinds who was Chair. This was an umbrella development organisation for the Saturday Schools Movement. Melvin Ellis also played a key role with his support by driving the minibus to pick up our children from the estates like Hockwell Ring and Marsh Farm.

Bob was also involved in founding the Luton Caribbean Heritage Group, who developed the Luton Black Community Award events. He dedicated an award to Eileen Williams in the Education category, and named it after her. Others who made a contribution at the time were Eileen's brother, Mr Terrelonge, along with community activist Zippy Bravo, who supported Bob and other community activists.

In 1981, I had started community cricket and football matches with the Bedfordshire police force in an effort to bring back the peace after the uprisings in Luton. Bob then turned the event in to a cricket 'world cup' with community matches between a local Indian, Pakistani, West Indian and English teams. I was able to assist Bob by providing a Test cricketer to cover each of the four countries. The first year I managed to recruit Gordon Greenidge from the West Indies, Derek Randall from England, Ajay Dajeda from India and Mushtaj Mohammad from Pakistan.

Before one official community match with the Police, Lawrence Palmer and his men from the Gemini Sound System challenged a very talented Starlight Youth Club cricket team with the likes of Kenroy Mingo and Alford Jackson. Afterwards, Lawrence stated:

"The one thing that stands out for me was the community cricket where there was a team from the youth club and the Gemini team which was made of people from the local sound system. It was attended by the local community at Sundon Park and you (Steve) bought a shield and trophies that was given out at the youth clinic in the evening. I went to the club which I saw as part of the community as a youth, and then later on I became the leader of the club."

BETRAYAL IN THE PROMISED LAND

My first negative experience of how the media behave against the Black community came in 1982. I was at the Starlight, minding my own business, when a researcher from Anglia television came into the club. He asked if he could do some interviews and carry out some filming for a documentary on the Caribbean community in Luton. I was happy for this to happen because it would give both me and the other community leaders in Luton a chance to portray our community in a positive light.

I was interviewed in the club and amongst other things I spoke about the social and psychological effects of Black youth unemployment. My friend Francis Reid, who was a senior member of the club, also gave a positive interview. He said afterwards that they filmed about four takes before finishing his interview. The documentary was entitled 'Promised Land' and we all waited in great anticipation for the television premiere. However, before the broadcast the researcher came to see me looking quite crestfallen. He was very apologetic and told me that they had to edit the programme and that some of the interviews were taken out. I said that was okay as I understood that a lot of filming took place around Luton, and they could not include everyone and everything.

However, when the programme was aired it came over with many negative stereotypes. They paid some young people to film several dances that were called 'Stubbins', and also focussed on a young Black woman claiming social security benefits who spoke about how she liked to receive the cash with her benefit book. There was only one positive part that I could recall when Derek Spaulding took them to the Bury Park area of the precinct, near what is now the Dutchman Pub, and he talked about the needs of the community in that area.

THE BEDFORD 13

In 1985, a member of the Starlight Youth Club had a quarrel with his girlfriend who was living in Bedford. This young man and some of his friends were members of the Church of God in Christ (Calvary) in Dallow Road, Luton. They took the church van and thirteen members of the youth club went and smashed up his girlfriend's house in Bedford. Several of the older boys were then charged with criminal damage of a council property and were remanded in Ashford Prison.

I was then a member of the Court Work team in Bedford, and I had direct access to the cells under the Magistrate's Court. I used to go down to the cells whenever these youths came into court, and give them two cigarettes and one pound each. This is something that would be quite unacceptable today. On one occasion when they came to court I was out of town on a case, and they were all remanded back to Ashford. I was then confronted by one of the boys' mothers who blamed me for his remand. Of course I explained to her that I was just supporting the boys on a voluntary basis, and that I had no say in their remand.

I then went to the One Foundation Organisation Saturday school when they had an evening meeting. I addressed about thirty parents and explained to them about the unfair treatment I had received from a disgruntled parent. I told them that I noted that some adults in the town were trying to blame the Starlight Youth Club for their children's behaviour. I put a question to the parents and asked them what they had been doing with their children from birth to sixteen years of age. It seemed to me that the majority of young people who arrived at the club had issues and problems that developed long before they came to us. A few of these youngsters told me that they were let out of the house early in the morning, and could not go back until the parents returned from work. I had been trying to support and help many of them to be responsible adults. When I had finished, I received a positive reaction from the majority of the parents, but some were not happy with what I had to say.

THE ASIAN CLUB

During the period when I was running the Starlight Youth Club, I was aware that the Asian young people did not have a youth club of their own. I therefore agreed with the Youth Service that the Bangladeshi community could use the space on Sundays, and the Pakistani groups had the Thursdays. It also turned out that we more or less ended up with a predominantly Asian club on a Saturdays as well.

I had set up this Saturday club to keep Black, white and Asian young people away from the notorious football fans who mainly came from London and used to plague the town centre area. After a few running battles with local youths, I started showing two kung fu movies every Saturday afternoon to entice the locals into the club. This was the heyday of the martial arts icon, Bruce Lee. I used to rent both the videos and a recorder so that I could show these films. By way of contrast, the Caribbean boys appeared to be more interested in the music of the sound systems that played in the club each Saturday evening. I therefore ended up with a group of about thirty Asian boys and a few white boys, who sat quietly and watched the movies every Saturday afternoon.

One Saturday I was not able to rent a VHS recorder, so I suggested that we have a table tennis, table football and pool competition instead. One Asian boy suggested they split into Sikh, Hindu and Muslim teams. This was a surprise to me, because although I was aware of the different religions, I had no in-depth understanding of their cultural differences. However, when the boys split up, it turned out that physically the Pakistani boys were taller and stronger, so I ended up having to mix the teams to give everyone a fair chance.

VENOL KING AND KYLIE MINOGUE

I am delighted to say that a number of those who attended the Starlight went on to greater things. A member of the X-Factor group *Voices with Soul* started her singing career at the youth club. The former amateur boxer, Renard Ashton was the first person to pay his membership to the club, although he did not become a regular member. In addition, former Tottenham Hotspur footballer Mitchell Thomas often attended the dances on a Saturday night.

One of the young people who I was most proud of was Venol King, who became pop star Kylie Minogue's personal choreographer and trainer from 1989 to 2004. Although I don't take any credit for his great achievements, it is important to tell this positive story of another of the club's former members.

Venol was a multi-talented individual who could have made it as a professional cricketer or footballer if the circumstances had been right then. He started playing cricket for the Bedfordshire under-14 team and also played for the youth club against the Bedfordshire Police and for Luton United. In addition, he played football for Ebony Starlight FC whilst I was the chair. When he was fourteen years old, Venol had a cricket trial at Northamptonshire CCC and he clean-bowled the former England player David Steel. This was no mean feat because many Test bowlers had found it difficult to remove Steel from the crease! Venol was told to come back when he was older, but his father felt he should learn a trade since being a young Black man then it was very difficult to succeed as a professional cricketer. So he did not receive any support from his family.

Whilst on a cricket tour to Germany in 1978, myself and several others spotted that Venol had another talent as a dancer. A Trinidadian soldier named Tony Ali from the second battalion of the Royal Anglian army based in Kent had invited Luton United to East Berlin. Tony played against United and was very impressed with the cricketing talent of the players. During the trip, the captain Ossie Clarke said to me one Saturday evening, "You are the youth worker; please take the young members of the team when you are going into the town". Luckily, we had a soldier named George from Grenada who had adopted us during the tour, and he took us to a night club in Stoltenberg.

Alford Jackson, Kenroy Mingo, Andrew Antrobus and a few others came along together with Venol and me. When Venol hit the dance floor in the night club some of the German people stopped dancing and started watching him instead. When we came back to the UK several of us would encourage Venol to think about dancing as a career, as he was clearly extremely talented.

Venol went on to win the regional disco dancing championship in Luton, and then the UK and Channel Islands 6th dance championship in Leicester Square, London. In 1984, a group of youth club members including Albert Hunter, Stephen Hoyte and Errol Frater went with me to the Hippodrome to support Venol in the Malibu World Dance Championships. Although Venol came second we all thought he was the winner. I was told later that the photos taken with Venol when we went on stage to congratulate him were seen all over Europe. A few years later he met Kylie Minogue at Pineapple Studios in London, and started teaching and choreographing her dancing and singing.

Like many of the youngsters who came from the Caribbean after their parents had left them behind to grow up with relatives, the relationship with our parents, especially fathers, was not that strong. When Venol started working with Kylie Minogue, his father Wilstan John asked me to speak to his son as he felt that he would trust me as a youth worker. He bluntly said that Venol was earning good wages, better than the average person, but that he felt Venol was wasting his money. I had been using sports and education to channel young peoples' energies in the right direction, and I was therefore really happy for both Venol and Mitchell Thomas, the footballer, who had both achieved a level of fame.

Money was really the last thing on my mind, as one of my main priorities was keeping youngsters away from the detention centres and the police who were harassing them all the time. This was the era of the infamous SUS Law and young Black men were constantly being targeted. I can't remember the exact conversation that I had with Venol, but it would have been similar to what I usually said to young footballers: if you are making extra money, invest it in property. Mitchell, who was a cousin of Venol, subsequently showed me the first house he bought in Luton, and I was very happy for him.

Several years later I saw an advert about Kylie Minogue appearing at the NEC in Birmingham. I told my wife Pamela and said that I would phone the NEC to see if I can speak to Venol. I was told Venol was on stage and I left a message. At about 1.00 in the morning I received a call back from Venol who had not forgotten about me. The next day he took me to lunch and then to meet Kylie at the hotel they were staying at in Birmingham. I remember asking Kylie jokingly if Venol was smoking or drinking because I always told him not to, but she said he was not. This was a bit cheeky of me as although I did not smoke, Venol had always told me and the other cricketers not to drink so much after matches!

Venol and another dancer named Richard then visited our home. However, the icing on the cake for us as a family was when Venol took us to the NEC in Birmingham to the concert and Pamela, Simone and Andrea met Kylie and her parents backstage. I always remember a young disabled boy in a wheelchair saw us coming from backstage and his parents asked us to get Kylie's autograph which I was really pleased to do for this little boy.

Venol King continued to work around the world with numerous famous artists including Michael Jackson, Tina Turner, Prince, Take That and Boyzone. Now a professional personal trainer he is still working with all age groups.

CHAPTER FIVE

Education and Work

The last six months of 1980 was a very busy period of my life, and a turning point for us as a family. I had re-opened the Starlight Youth Club and also began my degree as a mature student in Applied Social Studies at Hatfield Polytechnic. Our youngest daughter Simone was born in September that year. When I was interviewed at Hatfield for my social work degree, they were not only impressed with my two 'O' levels in English and Economics and my 'A' level in Economics, but more so that I had been working at the Chrysler truck plant in Dunstable whilst studying part-time. Once I had been accepted by Hatfield I left my job at Chrysler to start the course, and missed out on a redundancy payment.

From the outset, a lecturer told me and Patrick Wallace – the only other Black Caribbean man on the course – that he did not believe we could get a degree with commendation. This was before the start of honours degrees, so a degree with commendation was the highest award available. I really can't remember the lecturer's name but his negative words spurred both Patrick and me to go to the library and put our heads down, determined to prove him wrong. After four long years of travelling from Luton to Hatfield, I finally graduated with a degree with commendation, and both of us averaged seventy per cent in all our exams and course work.

My wife, Pamela, and my mother, Pearl, attended my graduation ceremony. Pamela was beaming all day. Looking

Pictured with Pamela and my mother, Pearl, at my
graduation ceremony at Hatfield Polytechnic in July 1984.

back, I could not have achieved this without her support.
Pamela also planned a surprise party for me after
graduation which I really appreciated. One of the highlights
was her secretly inviting Virrol Liverpool to the party – the
only Black lecturer on the social work course. I had received
a lot of support from Virrol, who was from St Vincent. He
particularly helped with my thesis on Black youth
unemployment.

Pamela told me once that a lady at Vauxhall Motors
where she worked for a short time told her that she was
wasting her time working so hard and supporting me, while
I spent my time studying. In the end, Pamela had the last
laugh as through my studies we ended up in a house in the
upscale area of Riddy Lane near the old Bedford road in
Luton.

There were several individuals from Luton who
provided me with invaluable support during my time as a
student, and also when I later became a youth worker.

HANNIBAL KANDEKORE

Hannibal Kandekore, or Mr Kandekore, as I respectfully
called him, was one of my main mentors. He was a modest
but very competent individual who was the second leader
of the Starlight Youth Club and the first Black man to be
chairperson of the Luton Community Relations Council. On
many occasions I would spend time at his home 'picking his
brains' on a range of subjects. Mr Kandekore was an
academic and intellectual of the highest order, who was an
avid reader and always up-to-date on current affairs. Later
on, I was pleased to support and advise his children when I
became an experienced social worker. His son, Patrice
followed me to Hatfield Polytechnic – now the University of
Hertfordshire – and his daughter Judy also went into social
work. By drawing on my own experience I was able to advise
and help both of them in the first year of their courses.

DOTLYN PAUL

Dotlyn Paul (née McCarthy Williams), or aunt Dotlyn as
she is affectionately known, supported me during my time
at Hatfield Polytechnic when my supervisor at the Probation
Service office in Shire County tried to fail me on my first
placement.

I was offered a place on the two-year Youth and
Community course at Leicester Polytechnic, but I really
wanted a degree. During my first week, I was walking
through the building when I was stopped by an usher who
shouted out loudly, "Are you on trial here, which court are
you in?" I responded by saying that I was a trainee probation
officer, and the look he gave me was one of contempt! A few
days later another usher told me that I couldn't use the car
park, because it was only for members of staff.

These two examples clearly demonstrate the racial
stereotyping that existed then – if you are Black and go to a
court then you must be an offender! It is astonishing that
this type of behaviour is still happening over forty years
later. Alexandra Wilson, a qualified Black barrister, had a

similar experience in a London court in 2020. And two
current MPs have also suffered from this form of racism.
Dawn Butler, the Shadow Women and Equalities Minister
whom I met at a Jamaican Diaspora conference in 2008,
told me that she was once mistaken for a cleaner. Butler,
the daughter of Jamaican immigrants, said she was in the
members-only lift when an MP who she has never named
told her: "This lift really isn't for cleaners." The Labour MP
for Brent Central said it had been one of "so many incidents"
of racism she has encountered while in parliament. She also
said that in 2005 a minister challenged her for being on the
Commons Terrace which is reserved for MPs. She said he
remarked: "They're letting anybody in nowadays."

Abena Oppong-Asare, the new MP for the London seat
of Erith & Thamesmead, has also claimed that a
Conservative MP who saw her outside the Commons
chamber put his bag in her hands and asked her to look
after it, not realising she too was an MP!

JIM THAKOORDIN

Whilst I spent less time with Jim, he was one of my lecturers
when I was at evening classes studying economics. He
allowed me to visit his home and to borrow and read some
of his books. I am pleased that years later I was able to
return the favour for his daughter who was studying in
Glasgow, and I was able to send her some anti-racist
literature.

It is my personal opinion that these three people –
Hannibal, Dotlyn and Jim – with their education and
experience could have been senior managers/directors in
most public sector environments. However, one of the factors
that went against them, like me, is that they spent a lot of
their valuable time fighting racism, which is a very time
consuming business. This is something that our white
colleagues never understood. We all had to do our regular
jobs to a high standard, but at the same time we had to
challenge the inequalities in the workplace and wider society

and support the many vulnerable victims that we came across along the way. Unfortunately, some of the people I helped did not go on to support others when they were established as senior managers. Some, but not all, collude with the system in order to get promotion.

LOCAL GOVERNMENT

In February 1986, I left Bedfordshire Social Services and moved to Birmingham to join the fostering unit in Newtown, and became the first Black worker in the team. Due to my in-depth knowledge of the Black community, my manager, Vivienne Meadows, suggested that 'Race' be added to my job description, hence my job title was Social Worker (Race). After the uprisings in September 1985, the white social workers in the team did not want to visit Handsworth to recruit Black and Asian foster carers. I took off my tie and went to the Black and White café in Handsworth and showed some recruitment posters to a few young men and asked them to share them in the community.

One young man told me proudly that he had at least three different women in different high-rise flats in Lozells, and some of them might need to come into care. I was a taken aback by his comments, and although I was outnumbered by these young men, who would be described as dangerous by the system, I challenged him. I explained that this was not a joke since I was constantly witnessing Black children coming into a care system that was not meeting all their needs.

I gave him an example of how some Black children who were placed with white parents had lost their identity. They were ashamed to be Black and were rejecting the culture and heritage of their birth parents.

At that time we had what was called the 'trans-racial debate', the placement of Black children with white families which was for some a very emotive and controversial subject. Many Black children denied their 'Blackness' as part of a coping mechanism. The young man and his friends stopped smiling, and he said sheepishly that he was only joking and was sorry to hear about the children's experiences.

I went on to develop guidelines for use in carrying out Black and cultural identity work, which initially some Black social workers thought was overstepping the mark in relation to my role. However, on being told that my job title was Senior Social Worker (Race), they grudgingly accepted what I was trying to accomplish.

I felt that whilst they were taking an anti-racist stance they never thought about developing such an information-giving resource. However, I was also of the view that if we were going to critically analyse the work of the white social workers and the department as a whole, then we should offer solutions.

People in the Black Caribbean community used to make comments like, "You can spot some of the children who were in care, because their skin and hair is usually a mess." I therefore approached all the barbers and shops that sold Black hair and skin products and asked their permission to put them in a directory. They all agreed to be included and were happy to do this as it would generate more business. Some white social workers used to say the products are too expensive, but my reply was that Black people in the city also pay their rates and income tax.

Our team eventually became a team where the majority of the workers were Black. We were then labelled as too radical, but we used to say what they called 'radicalism' we called 'good practice'. It was no surprise that the work that we were doing became the norm.

My first big event for Birmingham City Council was a foster campaign to recruit more Black and Asian foster carers. I invited Ricky Hill, my footballer friend who played for Luton Town, to help launch our foster campaign. I not only recruited Ricky to be the special guest but also my two daughters, Andrea and Simone, appeared on all the promotional material with their hair in plaits. During the campaign a lot of people became fascinated with their hairstyle and encouraged Pamela and I to try and get them into modelling.

I then met with Cyrille Regis and Mark Walters who helped to support several campaigns in Bedford and Northamptonshire. By this time Paul Elliott was also involved along with Derek Redmond, the Olympic 400 metre runner, Jodie Hanson from the television soap *Brookside*, and Rudolph Walker from *EastEnders*.

Mark Walters' support was crucial. He is a quiet and modest individual but an extremely talented footballer who supported a lot of my events over the past 30 years. Pamela and I are godparents of his two children and we speak quite often. I was really sorry to hear in March 2021 that his beloved mother, Mrs Ivy, had passed away. Pamela and I used to stay at her house when we visited Birmingham and we were welcomed and treated to nice Caribbean meals.

In addition, I contacted John Barnes in Liverpool and his wife sent me a dozen autographed photos of John for children in care. I was reminded recently by a boy who was in care back then that I took him to Aston Villa Football Club where he met several of his idols. This young man is now a well-known journalist and still living in Birmingham.

In order to help with the Black identity work that I carried out with Black children in care, I commissioned a Black shop in Heathfield Road to make some Rastafarian, Sikh and Hindu dolls. I also went to Harambee Bookshop in Handsworth and ordered culturally appropriate books and set up a resource library for social workers. Later, Carver Anderson and Ranbir Baines joined the social work team and fully supported my work. I would like to add here that I am extremely proud of my friend Carver who is a devout Christian. He completed his PhD after many years of hard work. The Reverend Dr Anderson is still actively involved in Birmingham, working with disaffected young men who are part of the gang culture. He is an executive director of the Bringing Hope charity.

Carver and I were two of the first Black social workers to lecture and tutor at Birmingham Polytechnic where I set multi-ethnic questions for the course. The first was about Black children and identity: 'All children are the same and colour doesn't matter. Discuss'. The second was, 'Outline the development of the Rastafarian movement from the 1920s to the present day' which came about because a disproportionate number of Rastafarian children were coming into the care system. It was recognised that Birmingham had one of the largest Jamaican and Caribbean populations in the country at that time.

There were a small number of incidents in local government that I would like to share that really defined my career, mostly involving Black women.

Whilst our team was actively taking an anti-racist approach we also had some issues of prejudice in our own community that needed to be addressed. A young Rastafarian mother was going into hospital for a few days and her two daughters aged three and six had to come into care. The mother arrived at the home of one of our Black foster carers, knocked on the door and the foster carer shouted, "Oh no, I am not taking these children with their dirty locks". The young mother was understandably quite distraught. I visited the carer and told her that her behaviour was insensitive and unacceptable. She turned to me and said, "I don't mind you coming to my house; you are well groomed with your hair trimmed". Of course, we subsequently struck this woman off our list of carers. If this had been a white foster carer we would have said this was racism, but unfortunately we have people in our own community who have been prejudiced against Rastafarians who are a minority within a minority. Some people are not conscious that they hold such prejudices, and they require what I would call Black awareness and Black empowerment training.

I had another situation at Birmingham Polytechnic whilst working there as a lecturer. I had set some examination questions and went to the reception to collect the papers for marking. A Black woman came to the window and said, "You can't have the papers, we can't have mature students collecting examination papers". I was shocked and informed her that I was a senior social worker and lecturer. She gave me a long stare and then offered an apology saying, "Sorry, I have never seen a Black lecturer before". This woman had actually internalised the institutionalised racism of the polytechnic, because as far as she was concerned all the lecturers were white.

The incident that led to me, Carver Anderson and many other Black workers taking a stand occurred when a Black woman attended the Black workers support group which was about 300 strong, with most of them being unqualified social workers. There were only four Black senior social workers at that time; myself, Christine Kelly, Thelma Hoare and Delroy Pommel, and we spent a lot of time mentoring and supporting Black staff, many of whom were vulnerable. The woman in question claimed that she had been dismissed for a trivial reason as her manager did not like her. During this period it was quite common that if your face did not fit or if you were known to be a member of the Black workers group and adopted an anti-racist stance, managers and other colleagues viewed that as a threat. Being unqualified rendered those workers in a weaker position and whilst most people said nothing to our faces they would undermine us in a covert way.

At least one hundred Black colleagues went on a march to Birmingham City Council House to demand the re-instatement of the worker. I spoke on the local radio station and criticised the council's equal opportunity policy. Several months later I applied for an assistant-manager's post but did not get the job. To my surprise, a colleague with less experience was appointed. I had been in my post for nearly four years, and this individual only had 18 months' experience. This person had often visited our office for support from myself and my Black colleagues. She appeared to be a bit embarrassed when we later met, but I wished her well and did not hold it against her. Although I did not get the job, the feedback was that I had a good interview and came over as very confident. Later, I was told in confidence by a white manager that one of the reasons for not being appointed was the fact that I was too close to the Black community!!

Following the 1988 hurricane Gilbert in Jamaica, I became joint-coordinator of the Birmingham Hurricane Disaster Fund, and worked closely with Steve Batchelor who was the manager of the Afro-Caribbean Centre in Winson Green. I was often challenging the council and other public bodies to improve the services for our community and was advocating the same issues as Steve.

Some of the council managers noted that I had an article in the *Birmingham Evening Mail* whilst joint-coordinator. However, I helped to raise £25,000 which for Jamaica was the largest sum they received from any city in the UK. My fund raising efforts included swimming 100 lengths in Newton Swimming Pool with a social work colleague named Maria, and afterwards I was interviewed on Jamaican television. I also made an appearance on Central Television for a foster campaign to recruit Black and Asian foster carers, and I duly gave my fee to the Disaster Fund. In some people's eyes it was clear that I was not management material because I was obviously too close to my own community! This was a joke as in my time in local government I knew white senior managers who sat on committees of all white voluntary organisations, and no one ever thought to object!

Another case that particularly sticks in my mind was a situation where a Black female social worker went on a visit to a foster carer. On arrival she heard the partner who was fostering with his wife shout, "Come on Nigger, come on Nigger!" The man was, in fact, calling his dog by the name he had given it! The social worker told him this was offensive and they agreed that they would change the name of the

dog, but did not. After a second visit she complained to the
assistant director who invited us both to a meeting to discuss
the issue. We agreed in the meeting that he would contact
the family and discus the changing of the name which was
never done, and the woman took the council to an
employment tribunal for racial discrimination.

At the time, I was off sick with a whiplash injury
following a car accident, and gathered that senior
management were pleased that I was not at work. However,
when I met the complainant she had not only lost weight
but was clearly affected by the stress of the case. I therefore
made the decision to try and attend the tribunal which was
going to be held in my home town of Bedford. My doctor
gave me permission to attend, as long as I wore a surgical
collar. My statement in the witness box helped the woman
to win both the case and substantial compensation.

Interestingly, I noted that during the hearing of the
case the senior manager denied any knowledge of the
agreement that we had made in the meeting. I know I was
telling the truth so I asked to swear on the Bible when it
was my turn to give evidence. Several years later a person
who was on the panel of three told me that the chair was
impressed when I asked for the Bible.

In all of these cases I simply stood up for what I believed
was right. In the first place I was denied promotion unfairly,
the second contributed to being made redundant although
the council would not admit it, and in the third case it was
felt that I was challenging the council in various reports
and meetings, with little support from managers. I heard
on the grapevine that this did not go down well with senior
management, and not long afterwards they contacted me
to say that my post was no longer available due to
redundancies in the council.

A few weeks afterwards I received a call from a manager
at Bedfordshire Social Services Kingsway office who were
seeking a senior social worker with experience of working
with the Black and minority ethnic communities. I fitted

the bill, applied, got the job and returned to Bedford in August 1990.

The four years I spent in Birmingham were very fruitful in the sense that I achieved a great deal, both in my job and with my voluntary and charity work. I remember visiting a Saturday school run by Rosemarie Campbell as part of 104 Heathfield Road where Beanie Brown, a well-known community activist, was one of the leaders at the centre. I was able to get a small grant to help the school.

The first person I liaised with in Birmingham was James Hunte who ran the Mohammed Ali Centre in Hockley where I first met Stedman Wallen who is mentioned elsewhere in the book. I was asked by the police to join the Handsworth Police Liaison Panel, and was a member of the Handsworth Employment Scheme. I liaised with Hyacinth Osborne at Birmingham Race Equality Council and the Asian Resource Centre in Villa Road. I later became a member of the Institute of Jamaica, now known as the Association of Jamaican Nationals led by Dr Beverley Lindsay and in 1989 helped to write the constitution at the FCF Club in Soho Road along with Hyacinth Osborne, Steve Batchelor and Basil Clarke. Gus Williams, a director of ACAFESS, was also a member. In 1987, Steve invited me and my wife Pamela to what was a confidential meeting with fourteen other community representatives where we met the great Michael Manley, a former prime minister of Jamaica.

Although there was a negative side to moving to Birmingham it was also a turning point in my life and career since this is the period when I met both Mark Walters and Cyrille Regis and established a strong link with the West Indies cricket team. I was one of the few people who had access to the West Indies changing room during matches and was able to get autographed bats on a regular basis which were auctioned for up to £300 each.

I recall that Clive Lloyd allowed me in to the changing room at Edgbaston cricket ground during a Test match. I had previously spoken to Clive at a charity match at Aston

Manor in Birmingham about issues in the community and was impressed with his level of awareness from the work he was doing in London and nationally. Clive's kindness led to me getting involved in lots of sports and charity work.

I attended Villa Park every Saturday and was given access to the players' lounge mainly because of my friendships with Paul Elliott and Mark Walters. Paul had joined Aston Villa about six months before I started working in Birmingham, so when he mentioned that he was staying on his own at the Albany Hotel in the city centre Pamela invited him for dinner. Paul used to come to our house on most Thursdays, and one day he brought Mark Walters with him as he was just living around the corner.

As a result, I was able to get signed footballs at Aston Villa and also when Mark went on to play for Liverpool. On one visit to Liverpool to see Mark play, John Barnes gave me a signed Liverpool football that auctioned for £300, which was a lot of money in those days. The money was used to buy cricket gear for Jamaica's under-15 team. John and Cyrille Regis also gave me sponsorship money which I used for the 'Man of the Match' for Birmingham Cavaliers when they played in the VM Cup and Clive Lloyd Cup.

SOCIAL WORK AND ANTI DISCRIMINATORY PRACTICE (ADP)

Following the incidents described above and the unfair way I had been treated for supporting others in an anti-racist and anti-discriminatory stance, I decided to investigate whether things had improved with regard to anti-racist practice in social work. In 1989, the Central Council for Education and Training in Social Work (CCETSW) made the following statement which was never really implemented, but had been much discussed by social workers like myself who were hoping for change:

> "Social Workers need to be able to work in a society which is multi-racial and multi-cultural. CCETSW will therefore seek to ensure that students are

prepared not only for ethnically sensitive practice but also to challenge and confront institutional and other forms of racism." (Dip SW Regulation Paper 30, 1989)

In a 1990 article in *Social Work Today*, Peter Fern had said that, "Attempts to tackle racism in social work training have met with little success. The most enduring and widespread response to racism on social work courses were apathy. It ranges from the crass 'we don't have any Black people on our course so racism is not a problem'... to the sophisticated 'we have got an equal opportunities policy statement and we have set up a working party, so it's been dealt with.'"

I hasten to add that from my own experience this is not just about social work. I have heard the same or similar comments in other council departments, as well as other public sector organisations, especially whilst attending seminars and conferences.

Fast forward to January 2021 when I came across an article by Wayne Reid in the *British Association of Social Workers (BASW)* journal. The article published on 16th December 2020 once again highlighted the fact that little had changed, and asked that action replaced questions about anti-racism in social work.

How ironic it seems because I used to make similar statements in the 80s and 90s whilst lecturing and speaking at seminars. My key points were that we didn't need any more legislation, we didn't need any more research and most of all we don't need any more excuses! Wayne Reid continues:

"Social work is institutionally racist and there has been a lack of explicit action to tackle this post-George Floyd and Black Lives Matter. It's time for meaningful action that results in systemic change...The legal backdrop and framework is built on the Human Rights Act 1998, Race Relations Act 1976, Disability Discrimination Act 1995, Sex Discrimination Act 1975 and Equality Act 2010. Therefore, it's almost

incomprehensible in my mind that these hard-fought
principles are omitted from today's regulatory
standards and supplementary guidance."

There is little that I can add to his incisive comments about
the current state of affairs. The current social work
standards are regressive and do nothing to advance the
principles set out by their predecessors – despite the
desperate and obvious necessity. Many believe these
principles are now diluted and de-prioritised beyond the
point of complacency. Similar concerns have been raised by
the chief social worker for children and families, with
regards to the teaching of anti-oppressive practice in a social
work education.

Unfortunately, the challenges of being a social worker
in today's world of high caseloads, blame culture and basic
survival, understandably mean that activism and unity have
declined in social work practice.

Now the pendulum has swung the other way due to
weaker trade unions, 'managerialism', specialisation of
services, high profile scandals, austerity, excessive
paperwork and greater individual accountability.

The social work magazine, *Community Care*, reported
that Black and ethnic minority social workers are "over-
represented in fitness to practice cases, and adjudication
hearing panels are disproportionately white compared to
the profession."

A CHANGE OF DIRECTION

I came out of social work practice in 1992 and went into
policy development in the equalities field. My first role was
Principal Officer Ethnic Minorities for Northamptonshire
Social Services. My interaction with local social work
managers was mostly positive, but in another shire county
it was rather more negative as when managers discovered
that I was a qualified social worker they accepted me as a
person, but not my role as Principal Equalities Officer. I was

asked to carry out a two-part presentation, but after my first talk I was not invited back. I was told later by a Black social worker that they did not like my presentation but this was not my own work that I had presented. All I did was present the findings from the Macpherson report into the murder of Stephen Lawrence. Despite the fact that the council had a legal duty to promote race equality under the Race Relations Amendment Act 2000, they did not really want to know!

Between 2009, when I returned to social work, and December 2018 when I left social services for good, very little was done or said about race. I was told by a manager and some social workers that they felt uncomfortable working with Muslim families although I did not believe that any of these workers were racist. They said they worried about making mistakes or saying the wrong things. I recalled a case where one social worker had set up a meeting with a Muslim man for a Friday at 1pm and the gentleman did not turn up. I reminded her that Muslims attended Friday prayers (Jumah), a day of worship in Islam. So the fact that he didn't turn up was in no way a reflection upon her. I also reminded some of the workers in my team to be especially mindful during the Muslim holy month of Ramadan and also during the Hindu festival of Diwali.

If social workers had a case with a family in the Black, Asian or minority ethnic community, they always tried to provide an ethnically and culturally sensitive service, and they would ask Black social workers like me for advice. However, if there was any racism from clients, managers did not want to address it. A Black social worker told me once that whenever race was mentioned in supervision it was quickly shut down.

RACISM IN EMPLOYMENT

I have identified with my colleague Maxie Hayles from Birmingham who stated in a *Gleaner* newspaper article of December 2020 that he was not considered for certain jobs because he 'spoke out' and was labelled as a trouble maker.

Having had similar experiences, no one has ever mentioned to my face that I was a trouble maker. I applied for several jobs in the voluntary sector that were not in the equalities field or social work, but with no success. Yet, in addition to my social work qualifications, I am the holder of an NVQ Level 5 in management. I applied for at least five different jobs and on every occasion was told I either finished second or had a very good interview. For one post, I was interviewed twice and was still not given the position. Later, a friend informed me that the person who got that job did not have half my level of experience. I found out this was true when I came across this person in another role. In another interview I was told that it was close, and on another day I would have been employed. In all of these posts it was a white person who was appointed!! Colleagues of mine who knew some of the individuals who got the jobs kept telling me that I had more experience than those who got the positions. It would appear that my experience was not seen as an opportunity to work with me, but rather was viewed as a threat.

In the 1990s, I had challenged a council and other public bodies at a meeting in a shire county. Soon after I applied for a job in the health service and was not successful, despite having a very good interview. A few years later someone who worked in the health service told me that they felt I was 'too radical'. I remember at the interview calling for an interpreting and translation service to be developed. Is that perceived as too radical? What they perceive as radicalism I regard as 'good practice'.

In another situation which happened in the same county I was told six months later by a person who worked in the office in a voluntary sector organisation where I was interviewed that I came first, but was still not given the job.

Following the Black Lives Matter campaign, several celebrities and others have spoken out about their experience of racism in the UK. Whilst I applaud them for doing so, my utmost respect goes to my colleagues who spoke out before.

Quite a few people who previously kept quiet have praised me for speaking out over the years. However, this is little comfort to me, although I understood some people's position. As a qualified social worker it was always easy to get a job in child protection because of the on-going national shortage especially after the Baby P and Victoria Climbié child abuse scandals. Others were not so fortunate, and therefore chose to report things to me and some of my colleagues in the equality field, but were always afraid to take it further.

SUPPORT FOR BLACK WORKERS

There has been a lot of talk in the media from Black people saying there are not enough people looking like them in certain positions in the UK, and it's often said we need more Black people in positions of power to elicit change. With the advent of the Black Lives Matter protests, this has become even more evident. Unfortunately, it's not people like me who have stood with our community for over four decades that usually benefit with better jobs and promotions.

Due to my own experience, I have never fully agreed with this notion of having 'BAME' people in the right positions. Some of the Black and minority ethnic people who make it to the top of their professions have to 'play the game' to get there, and speak the language that the system wants to hear. And many feel unable to challenge the inequalities and injustices.

People in authority need to be competent and not 'set up to fail'. After the uprisings in 1981 and 1985 many local authorities employed more Black people using Section 11 grants to deflect criticism by local communities. This was Section 11 of the 1966 Local Government Act which empowers the Home Secretary to pay grants to local authorities and other institutions to support the cost of employing additional staff to help minority ethnic groups overcome linguistic and other barriers that inhibit their access to take up mainstream services. During this period, the greater part of the funding was allocated to education. This grant covers 75 per cent of staffing costs, with 25 per cent borne by the local authorities.

These Black, Asian or minority ethnic individuals would then deliver a service to their community as mainly race equality advisers, youth and community workers as well as unqualified social workers. However, many people got into their posts only to discover that there was not enough support. On many occasions they had no administration, no proper office space, little or no budget and were managed by mostly white managers who did not understand how to support them and meet the needs of the Black community they were meant to serve. We are now in 2021 so I hope that when Black people are given a chance to shine in the future they don't come up against the same barriers.

During my entire career in local government I have never received support from any senior Black managers, except for Valerie Grant who was head of equalities in Bedfordshire. If they had intentions of doing so, they would probably have to do it in their own time and outside the workplace. This is how I have supported many people to become qualified social workers. Those who tried to do this in the workplace would have been told that it's not in their remit. I have consulted with several of my former colleagues, who confirmed that this was their lived experience too.

For example, in most local authorities they behave in a certain way if there is a Black workers' group. Senior managers are always secretly monitoring attendance. Some senior Black managers or aspiring managers will attend the odd meeting to deflect criticism from the Black workers' group, but they usually stay under the radar and when promoted rarely attend again. Whilst they have done well on a personal level and I respect their achievements, they are not able to support Black colleagues or their community whenever there is a controversial issue relating to a public body. They are conspicuous by their absence, and they always seem to have a good excuse for non-attendance.

If organisations in the public sector are going to use positive action measures from the Equality Act 2010 to redress the imbalance, they will have to develop and put the proper infrastructure in place to support people from the Black, Asian and minority ethnic communities.

Another key issue is that of the role Black social workers and the attitude that some of them have about being identified with their own community. Some see this as marginalising them and resent being thought of as 'the Black expert', whereas in reality they are simply the social worker who happens to be Black, and furthermore were Black before they became a social worker.

I get the impression that it was often just a lack of confidence that brought about this attitude, and at times they also had to fight their own battles with racism. They would say privately that they were concerned, but felt that if they became an advocate for other Black social workers and/or our community that it would affect their career progression. Some would also cite the fact that they had struggled on their own to get where they are. When I was supporting people to become qualified social workers, I always said I hope they go on to support others in a similar situation, but unfortunately a few forgot where they had come from!

ASHANTI HOUSE

I returned to Luton in 1999 and worked for social services again as manager of Ashanti House – a project for Black and Asian people with mental health issues. The council had wanted to close it, but after being there for six months the assistant director in charge of the project was impressed with my contribution, especially the finances, and decided to keep it open. So I helped to save Ashanti from closure. In this role the skills I learnt from my NVQ Level 5 in management training were very useful, although just understanding Black culture and the Black community would have been enough.

During this period I worked closely with Patrick Markland who was chair of the local African Caribbean Development Forum. Patrick led a campaign to get Caribbean food served at the Luton and Dunstable hospital and I supported this campaign, along with Bob Baker and others who worked to bring about this change. Patrick and the forum have continued to make a positive contribution to community in Luton.

Another interesting situation occurred when I went to a mental health conference at the Cranfield Institute in Bedfordshire. During one of the plenary sessions, I told the large crowd in attendance that having been at Ashanti House for nearly eighteen months there had not been one incident of aggression or violence from those attending the service. There has always been this racial stereotype about Black people, especially Black Caribbean men being violent and aggressive. In the lunch break a few health care professionals, including doctors, spoke to me and some looked surprised by my comments. I just used one word to them and this was, 'respect'.

I went on to say that we have some people, mostly African Caribbean men, who look dishevelled and their appearance suggested that they needed a shower on their arrival at the centre. However, whatever their physical condition and demeanour we welcomed them and looked after them. Once they noticed that we as members of staff understood and were sensitive to their needs, they relaxed and became more talkative.

Another situation involved a Rastafarian man who used to stand at the top of Market Hill in Luton town centre shouting obscenities, which people obviously found very offensive. I spoke to Bernard Abbey who was the youth worker at the Starlight Youth Club at the time. Bernie gave me some background information, saying he was probably suffering from mental illness and needed help. I decided to take a chance and went to Market Hill to see him. We met, and by using some Rasta terminology I instantly made a connection as he responded in a very positive manner. After introductions, I invited him to Ashanti House and he agreed to come. I got the impression that he recognised me from the time I was leader at the Starlight.

He came to Ashanti and we made him welcome with Caribbean food and drink. After a fairly long conversation, he broke down and cried explaining that he had a daughter, but had not seen her for a long time. I promised to ask Keith Heamans, one of my social workers, to try and make some enquiries. I left Ashanti House soon afterwards and heard that he had made a decision to cut his 'locks' and was also making good progress.

This is another example of how professionals should treat people from a different background and culture that have been wrongly labelled as violent or aggressive. I know that being an African Caribbean male helped, but it was my sensitive and respectful approach and showing empathy that really made the difference.

COMMUNITY WORK IN OTHER AREAS

Wherever I worked I always tried to make a positive contribution to the Black, Asian and minority ethnic communities. During my time in Birmingham I not only helped to recruit more Black and Asian foster carers than ever before, but also worked with the council's Black Workers' Support Group. We advised the council on the setting up of separate facilities for African, Caribbean and Asian elders, which resulted in other projects such as Annie Wood House. Annie Wood Golden Elders Group has now been running for over thirty years in Birmingham, and offers a chance for those over fifty, mainly from within the Caribbean community, to meet up and enjoy games of bingo and dominoes as well as to have coffee, tea and a chat on a weekly basis. An exercise session was also incorporated into the group for those who wished to take part.

My work in Bedfordshire and Northamptonshire was innovative in helping to introduce a new direction to race, social care and community development. Amongst other things in Bedford I initiated and developed day centre facilities for elders, mostly attended by Black Caribbean people. I worked initially at the day centre for Asian elders, and supervised four members of staff there.

Later, I trained and supported the Asante Project to start their first carnival in Bedford and also judged the floats. I attended the Handsworth and Leeds carnivals, and was asked to make a presentation at the latter. At that time, the St Paul's carnival in Bristol had not completed their race equality training, and the Arts Council threatened to cut their funding as a result. I designed a training package, and delivered it to their committee, thus ensuring the future of the carnival.

In Northamptonshire, I was involved in similar work. I was a member of a working party which developed two care management pilots for African, Caribbean and Asian elders, and assisted the setting up and development of the African Caribbean Centre (ACE) in Northampton in 1993.

I assisted in a large scale research survey with Ray Wright entitled: 'Care in the Community, How it Affects the Black Community in Northamptonshire', and collated and analysed the 1991 Census for the final draft of the report.

I moved to Wellingborough in November 2020, but have continued with my cases in the South West Region as well as nationally. Currently, I am the Regional Coordinator for the Eastern Region of the Jamaican Diaspora, and a member of the National Board. I was the previous co-ordinator for the South West Region. I am also the Senior Equality Officer on a voluntary basis for Friends of the Caribbean, based in Milton Keynes.

SUPPORT AND ADVICE

A lot of my current work has been carried over from the two periods I worked in Bristol and also from my role as a Senior Social Worker in Swindon. I was also the former Director of the Race Equality & Human Rights Service in Bristol. I inherited a lot of cases over the years, which I have continued to support.

I continue to advise and support several Jamaicans and Black, Asian and minority ethnic people in cases that are mainly race, immigration and Windrush issues, although I am also supporting several young cricketers, both in the UK and in Jamaica.

Recently, some of my work has been limited and restricted for various reasons including the Covid pandemic and foot surgery which led to my early retirement as a Social Worker. In addition there has been my daughter's cancer treatment, as previously discussed, and the simple fact that the South West Region is too large for one person to manage, especially after my colleague Pauline Reynolds resigned.

I have been a prominent member of the Jamaican Diaspora since being the first regional co-ordinator for the eastern region, and attended the very first conference in Jamaica in 2004. At that conference I was also elected to deputise for Travis Johnson who became chair for the northern region. Paulette Simpson and Barbara Ledgister were elected as chairs for the southern region.

Before the establishment of the Jamaican Diaspora I supported the Jamaica Welfare Fund at the Jamaica High Commission in London. I have worked with Delores Cooper and several High Commissioners over the years, most of whom have been regular attendees at the Victoria Mutual Cricket Cup annual dinner. During David Muirhead's tenure, I was given the privilege of reading the national prayer at St Martin-in-the-Fields church in London for Jamaica's annual independence church service in 2001. This was a proud moment for me and my family. My first cousin, Lee Rochester was extremely proud when I received the MBE from Her Majesty the Queen in 1996, and despite her failing health made it her duty to attend the aforementioned church service.

In addition, I worked with Delores Cooper, the community relations officer, in coordinating the visit to Swindon of Burchell Whiteman who was Jamaica High

Commissioner at that time. Delores asked me in November 2008 to support two Jamaican soldiers who were based at Watchfield in Oxfordshire which was only five minutes' drive from our home in Swindon. They were Major Kirk Johnson and Major Roderick Williams (now Brigadier).

On one occasion, there was an international food day with most of the Commonwealth and other countries being represented with their national dishes. The two majors wanted to make a Jamaican rum punch, but there no was Wray and Nephew rum available in the area. I stepped up and took a litre to the army base. We invited the two soldiers for dinner a few times and helped them with basic day-to-day things to help make their lives more comfortable. Both families loved my wife's Caribbean cuisine.

We have supported many Jamaicans and other people over the years, and have never asked for anything in return. However, the help and support we gave these families has been reciprocated when we have visited Jamaica, particularly by Major Johnson. For example, my friend, Courtney Walsh invited me and my family to a reception he was having at the Pegasus Hotel in Kingston for his foundation. I approached a taxi driver at the hotel who quoted me a substantial price by Jamaican standards for a return trip from the Bahia Principe Hotel in Runaway Bay, St Ann. I contacted Major Johnson and he came and collected us and then drove us back to the hotel late that night.

We have assisted Courtney and the West Indies team on many occasions, and Courtney chose that night to pay tribute to Pamela and me in the presence of over four hundred, including the former Prime Minister of Jamaica, P.J. Patterson. Pamela and I were very surprised and truly humbled. After the buffet meal many people approached us and offered thanks for the help we had given to Jamaican and West Indies cricketers.

Major Marlon Kennedy arrived in the UK in 2018 and we provided similar support to him during his stay. I then went to Jamaica in 2019 and was again in a difficult position in relation to transportation. Marlon collected me from my cousin Joan's home in Orange Grove, Kingston and took me to Ironshore in Montego Bay.

I would like to give a special mention to Gary Herbine, former Lucas CC and Jamaica youth cricketer, who played alongside Chris Gayle. 'Herbine', as he is affectionately known, has looked after me and acted as my bodyguard over the past fifteen years. We went out in Kingston nearly every night of the week, especially when Test matches were being played at Sabina Park.

Herbine played Under-15 cricket and was selected for the Jamaica Under-19 squad, but an injury curtailed any further progress. He was a promising all-rounder and could have made it as a professional.

I visited Jamaica in March 2020, just before the lockdown and had to return to the UK five days after entering the country. I went to Jamaica without a facemask (which were not easily available back then). Herbine took a bus ride from Kingston to Ironshore near Montego Bay and delivered a facemask for me to wear on my flight back to the UK.

My special thanks are also due to Philip Trenchfield and his wife for looking after me on many occasions when I stayed at their home in St Thomas. Philip is the former President of St Thomas Parish cricket club and Jamaica Cricket Board member. He is also the father of Jamie Trenchfield, the former Jamaican cricketer.

Philip is a businessman and a very knowledgeable individual, and we have spent many hours debating the state of West Indies cricket as well as current affairs. I have learnt a lot from this great man.

CHAPTER SIX

Racism in Schools

The first Black History Month celebrations took place in the USA at Kent State University in Ohio in 1970. By 1976, it had become a national event championed by the then President Gerald Ford. In the UK, Ghanaian Akyaaba Addai-Sebo is credited with starting Black History Month in London in October 1987, with Ansel Wong also being instrumental along with Herman Ouseley. With all due respect to Ansel, Addai and Herman, I was teaching Black history at the Starlight Youth Club in Luton way back in 1976! How this came about was as follows.

Franklin Hunter, Joseph Alexi and I had all attended a course run by Black history pioneer Sam Morris from Grenada. The course was held at the Luton College of Higher Education. In 1971, Bernard Coard who was also from Grenada, published a pamphlet entitled, *How the West Indian Child is Made Educationally Sub-normal in the British School System: The Scandal of the Black Child in Schools in Britain.* Coard had worked for two years as a school teacher in London, and ran several youth organisations in south London so knew exactly what he was writing about.

This pamphlet explained that British schools had a pervasive bias toward treating white children as normal, which led to many Black children being labelled as 'educationally subnormal'. Coard wrote that, "The Black children are therefore made neurotic about their race, culture and heritage. Some develop behaviour problems as a result due to such racist labelling and become resentful and bitter at being told their language is second-rate, their history and culture is non-existent; that they hardly exist except by the grace of whites."

Throughout the 1960s and 1970s, the presence of Black children in British schools was seen as problematic. Many Black children, particularly boys of Caribbean heritage, were routinely labelled as 'educationally subnormal' (ESN). Portrayed as unable to get to grips with the English language, suffering from a negative self-image and struggling with identity crises, many of these children were written off and subsequently dumped in ESN schools, where pupils were destined to be road cleaners and not much else. By 1970, in 'normal' London schools, 17 per cent of pupils were from ethnic minorities, but in ESN schools that figure was 34 per cent. Yet somehow racism was never believed to be the issue behind these shocking statistics by the authorities. Schools, local authorities and central government preferred to label the problem as a failure within the Black community and the Black family.

As a result I became a founder member of The One Foundation Organisation supplementary school in 1975, along with my friend Franklin Hunter. We attended the first meeting when the organisation was set up in Mr and Mrs McKoy's home in Luton, as I have previously discussed elsewhere. The organisation had already started classes at the Starlight Youth Club before I became the leader in June 1980.

I personally had already begun teaching Black studies and encouraged some of the young people to go back to college. When I started at the Starlight Youth Club in the mid-70s, many of the Black youth felt alienated and marginalised. Many of them were aspiring to adopt Rastafarianism, but had little or no understanding of the movement. During the same period Bob Marley had performed in London and at least one youngster from the club said he went to one of the concerts.

My own background had given me a good understanding of the issues. Whilst attending school in Kingston I was fortunate to have been taught Caribbean History and Geography for the Jamaica School Certificate (JSC is the equivalent to CSE in UK), which I was able to now pass on to my own students. A friend of mine had been in the band Count Ossie and the Mystic Revelation of Rastafari, and I used to visit Count Ossie's home as well as listening to Rastafarian reasoning in Wareika Hills near to Vineyard Town where I grew up. Because of this, I had some insight into Rasta reasoning about our history, and their views about people such as Marcus Garvey and Haile Selassie which I was also able to pass on.

More than 20 years later, Coard's findings were generally supported by new research carried out by my colleague Professor Cecile Wright, entitled 'Race Relations in the Primary School'. Wright had spent two years researching before producing her report in 1992. She had conducted an ethnographic study of four multi-racial inner-city primary schools. The study involved classroom observation of a total of 970 pupils and 57 staff; observation outside the classroom; informal interviews with all the observed teachers, some support staff and the four head teachers; interviews with the parent or parents of 38 children; and an examination of test results in three of the schools. Wright found that "the vast majority of the staff ... seemed genuinely committed to ideals of equality of educational opportunity". However, despite these ideals, there was still considerable discrimination in the classroom.

Fast forward again to 2004 and an official report stated that Black boys were three times as likely to be excluded from school as white boys, and the percentage of Black Caribbean pupils getting five or more grades A* to C at GCSE and equivalent was 36 per cent compared to 52.3 per cent of white children.

Coard's thesis has continued to be widely cited as a summary of the role of institutional racism in the relationship between race and intelligence. In 2005, it was republished as the central article in the collection entitled *Tell It Like It is: How Our Schools Fail Black Children* that was edited by Brian Richardson. How ironic that after thirty-five years, campaigners have seen fit to re-issue one of the first exposés of racism in the British education system. For racism and exclusion, if in new guises, still blights the lives of young Black people in Britain.

Coard's pamphlet aimed to expose the endemic levels of racism in Britain's education system and to rally communities to resist it. Yet clearly it is still as relevant today as it was back in 1971, as articles from politicians, academics and activists will testify.

RACISM IS STILL WITH US
So, more than three decades on, why has Coard's work been re-published? Because our schools are still failing Black children, is the simple answer. Although much has changed in education since the 1970s, too much remains the same.

According to Richardson, Black kids may not be labelled as 'educationally subnormal' these days, but they are disproportionately excluded from school, dumped in pupil referral units and sent into the world with fewer qualifications than their peers.

The statistics for exclusion of African-Caribbean youngsters, and boys in particular, has remained catastrophic. They are four times more likely to be excluded than any other ethnic group. Many are permanently excluded at the age of fourteen; so what then happens to them? They are out of school, have no qualifications, and are on the slippery slope downwards. Far too many end up in youth offender institutions and 'graduate' from there to prison where Black people are also disproportionately represented. This situation alone makes it a major crisis for the Black community, which will affect the society as a whole.

My social work colleague Ann-Marie Simpson sadly talked about being labelled ESN, and also how she had arrived in Britain at the age of nine with no relationship with her birth mother. This is a very common issue for children coming from the Caribbean during this period. In an article I wrote for the *Adoption Journal* in December 1987, I discussed how in the 1960s and 1970s the reunion of children with their parents in Britain after a long period of separation led to difficulties of adjustment. Not only did they have to adjust to a new society in which they were a very conspicuous minority, but also to a new family situation with perhaps a new step-parent, half-siblings and with no extended family to cushion the hardships. These were all significant stress factors. I have personally encountered similar situations that fit in closely with Bernard Coard's views, and the general racial stereotyping that continues to exist.

Following a Workshop in 2010 at the Jamaican Diaspora Conference at Bethel Centre in Birmingham, I made a brief presentation which related to Education. I told the audience: "When I was a social worker in Bedford, I was working with a Black Caribbean family. The family included a fourteen-year-old boy named Leroy. One day I received a phone call from a very overexcited teacher. He told me Leroy had broken both the 100 and 200 metres record at the school's sports day. I told him that this was really good but can he update me on Leroy's academic progress, because I am aware that he was under-achieving. The teacher went quiet and I could not hear a pin drop. He then sheepishly said that he would have to get back to me."

This was the sort of racial stereotyping we encountered, and when we called out teachers, some of them took offence. Later that day at the conference several professionals and parents praised me for highlighting this issue, because they had similar conversations with schools about pushing their children into sports and not supporting their educational development. I may have used sports as a vehicle for change throughout my professional career, but I always insisted that education was my Plan A, and sports my Plan B.

I remember being commissioned by Randolph Charles, who later became a councillor in Bedford, to run Black history courses for the Adult Education Department from March to May 1992. The courses were to last for six weeks in Bedford and then six weeks in Luton. I noted that several white teachers attended in Luton, which was very positive because they were working in schools with high numbers of African-Caribbean heritage children.

On another occasion, a white youth worker approached me at the Luton Youth House and told me that he did not like the attitude of a particular Rastafarian young man who attended the Starlight Youth Club I was then running. He compared him with another young man, with whom the Rastafarian had fought and told me the other boy was more intelligent because he spoke good English whilst the Rasta spoke Jamaican patois and did not came over as intelligent. I laughed a bit and he looked quite surprised. I then told him that the young Rasta had 'O' Levels, including English, and was actually quite intelligent. The other boy did not have any 'O' Levels as far as I was aware. I then told him the Rasta was 'blocking' him. He did not understand what this meant so I explained that he does not want to speak to you so he deliberately used Jamaican patois, even though he speaks good English. The youth worker was stunned by my comments, and clearly could not equate Jamaican patois with intelligence.

SOCIAL ENQUIRY REPORTS

During my years as a social worker I started to write Social Enquiry Reports for the Court. Prior to this time, many of the reports contained a lot of racial stereotypes and bias that went against Black families and their children. I was given a particular case with a white teenage girl and her family who were quite dysfunctional although I got on really well with them. This young woman was the leader of a small gang which included several Black boys, one of whom was her boyfriend. Before I wrote my report, I carefully read through the previous one. That report stated this young girl was running around with a gang of West Indian boys who were leading her down the wrong path. It was not correct because she was clearly the leader, and her boyfriend was merely following her. The report said he was West Indian, but actually he was not. I was also his social worker, and he came from a very respectable middle class West African family. His mother was a hard working business woman and they lived in a very affluent area. I would hasten to add that some of the other Black boys were no saints either, but they had to do as they were told by this dominant white girl.

BLACK CHILDREN AND IDENTITY

In an article I wrote which was published in the *Black Eye* newspaper in 2012. I examined the part English language and the media played in a Black child's identity. Many of the children were racially Black but culturally white; they also denied their Blackness as part of their coping mechanism.

I pointed out that the 'doll test' by Clarke and Clarke in the 1940s was replicated by David Milner in *Children and Race* (1975). Milner also conducted a follow-up in 1983. In 1975, he concluded that, "Black British children showed a strong tendency towards the dominant white majority and a tendency to devalue their own group. The evidence suggests that Black children internalised the racial values imposed by the dominant white group."

Forward to 2021, and whilst there is more recognition of race and culture I am not sure how much things have improved. I am only generalising here but I have met several Black British born individuals now in their 40s and 50s who told me they were confused about their identity in their teens, and are still not fully aware of their cultural heritage today! My daughter, Simone turned forty in 2020 year and told me she is aware of some Black people in her age group and slightly older who are still uncomfortable about being

Black. Part of the problem is where they were brought up and how they socialised as children. For example Arlene and Mark, my siblings, were born in the UK and have very positive images of their race and culture. Both of them went to the Starlight Youth Club where they had access to the Black Resource Library. Mark became a popular DJ in Luton going under the name 'Wareika', and used his skills to send a positive message to his audience who were mostly young Black people. However, contemporary psychologists say that Black children have now got better and white children have stayed the same.

Psychologist Margaret Beale Spencer of the USA re-created a questionnaire version of the 'doll test' in 2010 for CNN television, and found that while there was a 'white bias' in both Black and white kids, the bias was much less so in the Black kids. In other words, says Dr Welansa Asrat, a New York-based specialist in cross-cultural psychiatry, "The Black kids' self-perception has improved since the 1940s, while the white kids remained invested in the stereotypes." Today, psychology has better tools for measuring attitudes about race. The modern method of assessing attitudes on race is the Implicit Association Test, or IAT, which tests unconscious bias. According to a recent study, 70 per cent of whites have an anti-Black bias, as do 50 per cent of Blacks, says Asrat. The idea that integration is a solution to individual anti-Black bias has largely been dropped.

During the latest Black History Month I gave talks that covered the shameful trans-Atlantic slave trade. It was a particularly barbaric and grotesque phenomenon with a clear 'racial' dimension that nowadays sits awkwardly with the accepted belief in the equality and dignity of all human beings. However, the economic wealth of Britain and the industrial revolution was built and fuelled by the slave trade. In Britain there are many legacies of this despicable trade. Cities like Bristol, Cardiff, Liverpool and London all flourished from the trade in the 16th, 17th and 18th centuries. I understand that Birmingham also played its part by making chains and manacles that were vital to the trade in enslaved Africans.

Chattel slavery meant just that. The enslaved became commodities, cargo, just like the textiles, guns and other wares the slave traders handed over in exchange for them. Considered as property, their 'owners' could use them as they wished or murder them if they were too troublesome or too sickly, and without fear of prosecution. They were deemed as beasts of burden and not human.

The 25 March 2007 marked the 200th anniversary of the Act of Parliament that abolished the trade in enslaved Africans. Despite the civic commemoration of this important historical event, however, what most people do not know and many who do know fail to acknowledge is that the institution of slavery itself was not abolished in the British Empire until 1838. It is also rarely acknowledged that the trade in enslaved Africans was brought to an end not simply because of the moral outrage and religious conviction of white abolitionists, but because the enslaved Africans themselves revolted over and over again, risking their lives in the fight for freedom.

One of my papers entitled 'West Indies' was published in a 1987 edition of the *Adoption Journal*. A part of this article briefly discussed the effects and legacy of the slave trade and colonisation on the West Indian community in the Caribbean and United Kingdom.

BLACK LIVES MATTER

After the murder of George Floyd on 25 May 2020 in the USA, protests took place across the UK and around the world. People from all ethnic backgrounds shouted "Black lives Matter". This was not just Black people against racial inequality as it included those from diverse backgrounds.

The 2011 Census showed that the Caribbean heritage community makes up 1.1 per cent of the UK population, but we are disproportionally underrepresented in most areas of public life. However, where services are of a coercive nature we are over-represented such as mental health and also in the disproportionate use of 'stop and search' powers by the police. In addition, Ministry of Justice statistics on Race and the Criminal Justice System in 2019 showed that we are overrepresented as defendants. Of course, it goes without saying that where services are beneficial we are usually under-represented.

According to the Office of National Statistics, Black people living in the UK tend to be worse off than their white counterparts, with 22 per cent of Black children living in low income and materially deprived households. The national average is 12 per cent. Therefore, those that shout "all lives matter" don't see or understand the struggles of Black people, and even if they do they choose to ignore it. Even when Black people overcome barriers through education and higher education, they still have further problems to deal with. For example, the ethnic pay gap in London is 23.8 per cent. It is indefensible that in 21st century Britain, Black workers with degrees should earn almost a quarter less on average than their white counterparts with similar qualifications. This statistic was highlighted in the 2015 Equality and Human Rights Commission (EHRC) report entitled, 'Is Britain Fairer', and again in 'Healing a Divided Britain: The Need for a Comprehensive Race Equality Strategy', published in August 2016.

The historian and broadcaster, David Olusoga wrote in *The Voice* newspaper in November 2020: "If someone had told me that millions of young people around the world would organise thousands of marches and demonstrations in the name of anti-racism I would have dismissed the idea as fanciful". As an anti-racist and human rights campaigner for over forty years I fully agree with David. He added that the toppling in 2020 of the statue of 17th century slave trader Edward Colston that had stood in the centre of Bristol for 125 years, was a reminder that campaigners were unable to persuade defenders of the trader in human flesh to even agree to a plaque acknowledging the existence of the victims being attached to the pedestal on which the statue stood.

However, controversy over Colston's statue is nothing new, as the former director of the Race Equality & Human Rights Service (REHRS) in Bristol alongside Ayannah Griffiths CEO, and Marvin Rees, the current mayor, can testify. I recall having a conversation with Marvin, Ayanaah and others in relation to removing the statue and changing certain street names back in 2007. This issue came up whilst I was carrying out race equality and human rights training at the Black Development Agency (BDA) in Bristol.

It is interesting to note that whilst the statue was being pulled down, and with many people having their say on television and social media about the rights and wrongs of the action, veteran community activists like myself have quietly continued to support victims of race discrimination and the Windrush Scandal in Bristol. Since leaving that city in 2009, I have been back to the BDA numerous times on a voluntary basis to help my friend Ayannah with several race discrimination cases. I have often been approached by people on Stapleton Road when I go to the BRB Supermarket, owned by my long-time friend Errol Ballin, who has supported all my cricket events in Bristol. Many of them are still suffering from racial discrimination. I continue to support other people in Bristol in my capacity as regional coordinator for the Jamaican Diaspora South West region, which includes Bristol.

From March 2015 to March 2016, I was manager of the iconic Malcolm X Community Centre in St Pauls, Bristol. Now that the dust has settled, so to speak, is there going to be any further action and lasting changes from these protests?

The Black Lives Matter movement has raised many issues that are important for education. Currently, Black history is not taught as a curriculum subject in mainstream schools. Why is the education service avoiding this? 'Black

History is British History', and not only are Black children being deprived of it, but white children too need to be made aware of the past which impacts the present and has a bearing on the future.

Reverend Wayne Onkphra Wells from the Pan African Coalition of Barbados published an article entitled 'Reclaiming our human dignity' in *The Nation* magazine of January 2021. He stated that: "History cannot be sanitised to appease the conscience of the beneficiaries of such a cruel and inhumane system as slavery". He added that what those who are enjoying the affluence gained through that dread blood money should do is pay the appropriate reparation.

Onkphra went on to say, "European invaders often try to rewrite the scripts, change the narrative and rebrand their atrocities with acts of paternalistic benevolence. We the victims on the other hand are always more than ready to accepts their gifts, 'Trinkets to the Natives' and consider ourselves privileged, well on the way of social mobility while being trapped in a mental colonial schizophrenia."

The African proverb "Until the lions have their own historian, tales of hunting will always glorify the hunter" is an apt way of reiterating this all-important message.

Urban studies and diversity inclusion straplines continue to undermine Black history and are a panacea for confusion. What this says is that the teaching profession, like many other professions, is still uncomfortable about race and by extension racism. I have noticed on many occasions in seminars and conferences throughout this country, if you don't have a conscious Black speaker headlining this topic the panellists might mention race but they will do so only in passing with no in-depth analysis. If they are then challenged by Black people in the audience, they will sometimes sheepishly acknowledge that it's not covered in detail because of the pressure of time or some other notion. These people usually have a flimsy excuse for such an important subject, and can talk all day as long as it's not about race or racism.

It is said that an educated society is a tolerant society and the hallmark of an advanced civilisation is how the dominant prevailing culture treats others that are less privileged. However, Black history is more than just about Black people's pain and suffering. It's also about the creative genius of Black people collectively, including all the things we have invented. During slavery we could not patent any inventions, but since then we made a life from almost nothing.

MICHAEL HOLDING

Last summer my friend, former West Indies fast bowler Michael (Mikey) Holding, made a statement with regard to 'Black Lives Matter'. This has been one of the most important and moving statements I ever heard over the past forty years. In July 2020, a rain delay at the Test Match between England and West Indies at the Ageas Bowl in Hampshire gave Michael the opportunity to speak live on Sky Sports TV. Bryan Henderson, the CEO of Sky Sports, came up with the idea for both Michael and former cricketer Ebony Rainford-Brent to express their views on Black Lives Matter and racism in general.

Mikey spoke for the 'voices of the unheard'. In his powerful statement he looked up at the lighting at the Ageas Bowl and spoke about how Black people are denied recognition. He used the example of the light bulb by saying that most people might have heard of Thomas Edison who is credited with its invention, but how many people know about Lewis Latimer, a Black inventor and scientist, who helped to develop the electric light bulb. Latimer was also an artist, and an expert on the laws that cover inventions. In 1880, he went to work for the US Electric Lighting Company in Connecticut, and together with a co-worker patented an improved method for making light bulbs that allowed them to burn much longer. This was the point that Michael was making about the distortion of history.

Ebony also made a statement, and both I and members of our community were very proud of her contribution to an important debate. Whilst I was chair of the Victoria Mutual Caribbean Cup Competition we had given her a special award for services to cricket in 2007, as she was the first woman of African-Caribbean heritage to play for the England women's cricket team.

Before the speech, Mikey and I had been texting each other, and he had wished my daughter Simone all the best with her cancer treatment. I had also brought Caribbean food along to the Ageas Bowl for the West Indies team, following Coronavirus protocols. Both Mikey and Ebony really appreciated this food because of its scarcity during the lockdown.

After Mikey's speech I was inundated with messages of support for him, not only from the Caribbean cricket community in the UK, but the wider community all over the world. I then texted him to tell him his comments had gone viral and that he was receiving massive support.

I had played youth cricket in Jamaica during the same period as Michael Holding – 1966 to 1971. I have been calling him an icon for many years, but he would always modestly say he is anything but. However, after this, he cannot refute the fact that he is indeed thought of in these terms by a great many people.

There are numerous examples like the case of Latimer which was so eloquently highlighted by Mikey on that day. The obvious one that comes to mind is the case of Jamaican nurse Mary Seacole, and her British counterpart Florence Nightingale. Both Mary Seacole and Nightingale tended to injured soldiers during the Crimean War (1853-6), but Mary did not get the recognition she deserved because she was a Black woman. When she originally went to the War Office in London, requesting to join Florence Nightingale, she was turned down. Nevertheless, she got herself out to the war zone by her own means and expense, and risked her life to bring comfort to the wounded and dying soldiers, thus becoming the first Black woman to make her mark on British public life. But while Florence Nightingale has gone down in history as a legendary figure, Mary Seacole was relegated to obscurity until fairly recently. Through the unstinting efforts of the Black Cultural Archives and others her statue was erected in 2016 outside St Thomas' Hospital in Lambeth, London. So, nearly two hundred years later, Mary Seacole has found lasting fame for her work during the Crimean War and is now considered one of the greatest Black women in history.

In the 30th edition of the *Black Bright* magazine, I wrote the headline article entitled 'Black History Under Focus' which gave an example about the Black American explorer, Matthew Alexander Henson. It was, in fact, Henson and not expedition leader, Robert Peary who reached the North Pole in 1909, as the history books had stated.

Schools, if they are not already doing so, need to add Black history to the curriculum. How many people know that the West India Regiment was set up in 1795 and fought many battles alongside the British? A Black man named Benjamin Banneker was the main architect in the building of the White House in the USA. The phrase, "If you are not part of the problem you must be part of the solution" resonates with me, as I regard myself as part of the solution. I therefore suggest that we need to start with equality training for *all* public sector staff, but without rushing past race. Such training must focus on attitude and behaviour, and not just be an information-given exercise.

CHAPTER SEVEN

The Windrush Generation

The issues surrounding the Windrush Generation are now well known, but I have been praising and acknowledging members of those first arrivals in the UK for the past forty years. In Luton, I had a lot of support from many of the stalwarts of this generation, including my mother Pearl Stephenson, who spent most of her working life in the UK serving the Luton and Dunstable Hospital. Bishop Alvin Blake from the Church of God in Christ, Hannibal Kandekore, former chair of Luton community relations council, Valerie Taylor, a well-known community activist in Luton, and Dotlyn Paul (née McCarthy Williams), a good friend, university lecturer and a Black pioneer in social work, have all played pivotal roles as indeed have many others.

The arrival of the first group of 493 West Indian immigrants on the *Empire Windrush* was not expected by the British government, and more importantly, not welcome. George Isaacs, the Minister of Labour and National Service, stated in Parliament that there would be no encouragement for others to follow their example. In June 1948, eleven Labour Members wrote to Clement Attlee complaining about excessive immigration. In the same month, Arthur Creech Jones, the Secretary of State for the Colonies, noted in a Cabinet Memorandum that the Jamaican Government could not legally prevent people from departing, and the British government could not legally prevent them from landing. However, he stated the government was opposed to this immigration, and that all possible steps would be taken by the Colonial Office and the Jamaican Government to discourage it.

Although they were actively invited to Britain to help fill the many labour shortages after the Second World War, the government did not have a social policy to accommodate these new arrivals. In the 1950s, most Black immigrants who arrived in Britain from the Caribbean faced racism. For many Caribbean immigrants their first experience of discrimination came when trying to find private accommodation. They were generally ineligible for council housing because only people who had been resident in the UK for a minimum of five years qualified for it. Furthermore, there was no anti-discrimination legislation to prevent landlords from refusing to accept Black tenants.

A survey undertaken in Birmingham in 1956 found that only fifteen of a total of 1000 white people surveyed would let a room to a Black tenant. As a result, many Black immigrants were forced to live in slum areas of cities where the housing was of poor quality and there were problems of crime, violence and prostitution. One of the most notorious slum landlords was Peter Rachman, who owned around one hundred properties in the Notting Hill area of London. Black tenants sometimes paid double the rent of white tenants, and lived in conditions of extreme overcrowding.

Historian Winston James argues that the experience of racism in Britain was a major factor in the development of a shared Caribbean identity amongst Black immigrants from a range of different countries, classes and backgrounds.

Images of the African-Caribbean passengers filing off the gangplank have become part of the country's social history. The 1948 Nationality Act had granted British citizenship to those living in Britain's colonies, so, as British passport holders, this allowed Caribbean migrants to live and work in Britain. However, it emerged in 2018 that many Caribbean people who arrived prior to January 1973 and stayed permanently, were unable to establish continuous residence due to a lack of documentation. Many of these had now been wrongly detained, denied legal rights and threatened with deportation. In at least 83 cases they had actually been wrongly deported from the UK by the Home Office.

It was the Barbados High Commissioner Guy Hewitt's initiative that finally put the Windrush Scandal in the public eye, and led to the current compensation scheme. Hewitt, along with leading race relations campaigner Lord Herman Ouseley, the race equality think-tank Runnymede Trust, the Joint Council for the Welfare of Immigrants and Tottenham Labour MP David Lammy, drew up a timetable of events designed to force the issue on to the political agenda. Hewitt successfully coordinated the first ever press conference of all Caribbean High Commissioners at which they expressed dismay at the government's treatment of people who had lived all their adult lives in the UK. He concluded: "The UK is not at ease with race. People need to speak truthfully about Britain's colonial past".

The Windrush Scandal has become a British political disaster that continues to this day, as many are still waiting to have their cases heard or receive the compensation that they are due.

WINDRUSH LESSON LEARNED?
In March 2020, Wendy Williams wrote in the executive summary of her review, 'Windrush Lesson Learned' that, "Members of the Windrush generation and their children have been poorly served by this country. They had every right to be here and should never have been caught in the immigration net. The many stories of injustice and hardship are heart breaking, with jobs lost, lives uprooted and untold damage done to so many individuals and families.

While I am unable to make a definitive finding of institutional racism within the department, I have serious concerns that these failings demonstrate an institutional ignorance and thoughtlessness towards the issue of race and the history of the Windrush generation within the department, which are consistent with some elements of the definition of institutional racism."

In my opinion, Williams' words have overtones of Sir William Macpherson's famous definition of institutional racism. The Windrush Scandal, though, transcends an ageing group of mostly African-Caribbean Britons. It is largely a symptom of systemic racism against Black people and other minority ethnic groups in Britain, as was highlighted by the commission that reviewed Stephen Lawrence's brutal murder in 1993. It is now being highlighted again in the 'Black Lives Matter' demonstrations in the aftermath of the killing of George Floyd by a US police officer.

SCOTLAND, 1992

Although I have not been actively involved in the issues surrounding the Windrush Scandal, I have always felt that this generation's contribution to British history has been underrepresented and undervalued. As I mentioned earlier, I have personally tried to raise awareness about the situation of these first arrivals on many occasions, of which the following are just a few examples.

My first reflection about the Windrush Generation comes from when I was invited to speak at the British Association of Social Work (BASW) conference on 8 April 1992 in Inverness, Scotland. At the time, I was Principal Officer Ethnic Minorities for Northamptonshire Social Services.

Three people accompanied me on this trip: my manager Ian Winter who was an assistant director; a colleague Bert Cuff, a principal social worker; and Sue Mendez who was a community representative. Ian flew straight to Inverness whilst Bert, Sue and I drove by car from Northampton to Birmingham airport where we took a flight to Aberdeen airport and then a train to Inverness. It was the start of spring, and fortunately for us it was a warm and sunny day. I will never forget the journey from Aberdeen to Inverness. The scenery through the countryside and closer to the sea was breath-taking. I had previously travelled to Glasgow by car several times in the 1980s to visit Mark Walters, who was one of the first Black Caribbean footballers to play for Glasgow Rangers. The local scenery there was beautiful, but nothing could match what we saw on this train journey.

The title of my presentation was 'Black and White is not Grey', from which the extract below resonates with the Windrush Generation and is still relevant today.

"My father was one of the first of six West Indians to arrive in Luton, Bedfordshire, in the 1950s. My mother worked at the Luton and Dunstable Hospital for over 28 years. She is now 66, and now lives on her own whilst still working at this hospital. My mother-in-law coincidentally is the same age, but living in the Midlands and working in a similar job. They have all paid their taxes, rates and NI contributions over the past thirty years. However, now they are in need of services which should be theirs as of right, but there are no means for them to access the appropriate services.

They are now at risk through old age, through cultural and racial discrimination and through their lack of access to ethnically sensitive health and social care services. The facilities and service they need are not special, but additional, including the need to be meeting and socialising with their friends on a regular basis.

The presence of minority ethnic groups in Britain and their interaction with social services have raised many questions about social work values and methods. This, in turn, has implications for service delivery to minority ethnic groups whenever the needs arise. Many people would argue that the service is unable to cope. It is the failure to accept the role of racial discrimination as it affects social work training, administration and service delivery that has rendered the service impotent."

IN PRAISE OF CARIBBEAN ELDERS

My second contribution to the Windrush Generation came in the form of a book. In 1998, I interviewed 32 Caribbean elders, the majority of whom attended the African and Caribbean Elders Society (ACES) in Northampton. The book was the inspiration of my friend and colleague Olive Robinson who was manager of ACES. The book's title, *Cold Arrival: Life in a Second Homeland* has a double meaning. Firstly, many elders referred to the physical cold they felt when they first arrived in Britain, even during the summer months. Secondly, there was coldness towards them from the indigenous population and many were affected by their rejection.

The majority of the present generation of elderly people from the West Indies came to the UK in the period after the Second World War to help alleviate the severe labour shortages. Many of these original settlers intended to return to the Caribbean after a few years, but in so many cases they chose to stay.

The aim of this book was to provide historical and educational material which will give an invaluable insight into the strengths of Caribbean people. It is hoped that young people and other individuals locally and nationally will gain valuable insights from the stories of these remarkable elders. The true story of their contribution to Britain, during and after the war, is often ignored, and this book hopes to redress that imbalance.

With the support of Olive Robinson we used our creativity to create and write this book. During its development, I spent twelve months at the African Caribbean elders centre in Northampton. One of my main research methodologies was participant observation. As part of my preparation, I read and researched several books on Caribbean history which covered the slave trade. We then took the Caribbean elders to both the Slavery Exhibition in Liverpool and the Slave Trail Exhibition in Bristol. We took many photos during these trips, some of which are featured in the book. We also made cassette recordings of the elders' stories. A young woman of Caribbean heritage named Nicky Taylor also played her part, as my assistant and typist, during the writing of the book. Nicky then went on to develop the Northamptonshire Black History Month project. I developed the Caribbean quiz in the book.

During the project links were made with Wellingborough Race Equality Council which had done some earlier work recording and archiving the county's connection to the slave trade and the Caribbean.

I also participated in two archive projects in Bedfordshire. One involved recording the lives of the Black minority ethnic presence in the county, including my own story. The other was an oral history project which was recorded on radio and tapes and sent to the British Library for future generations to listen to and glean further knowledge.

NORTHAMPTON

My third contribution came on 18 September 2000, when I was the keynote speaker at the African Caribbean Centre annual dinner in Northampton. Afterwards, it was reported in *The Voice* newspaper that I had slammed the inadequate provision for ethnic minority pensioners, such as those of the Windrush Generation. This obviously did not go down well with some people in the council. The article mentioned that I challenged service providers to overcome racial stereotypes and institutional racism to meet elders' needs. I had added that many local authorities have assumed that the Black elderly are cared for by their own community but, as Olive Robinson stated, clearly their cultural needs were not being met elsewhere.

Little did we know just how much this generation would still have to face and deal with in the coming years.

CHAPTER EIGHT

West Indian Cricket

As previously mentioned, I have a long history of supporting West Indian cricketers, and hosting various functions for the West Indies team when they are in England. I have also supported the Jamaica under-15 cricket team for the past 30 years, as well as young Caribbean cricketers who played in England. I jointly managed Birmingham Cavaliers CC with my friend Geoff Pullar. The team was one of the most successful in the history of West Indian club cricket in the UK.

During my first visit to Jamaica in 1989, I met one of my boyhood cricket heroes, Easton McMorris, who had recently returned from the USA. Easton thought that whilst the players enjoyed the food and met with other Caribbean people, some of the events they attended were too long and with too many speeches. Following his advice I started all my events by letting the players eat first and kept the speeches to a minimum.

For most of these events I did not know the managers beforehand, but by the end of the tour we had become friends. Ricky Skerritt, now president of Cricket West Indies (CWI) board, sent me a special message on a CWI compliments slip which my wife Pamela and I really appreciated. Shivnarine Chanderpaul, Courtney Walsh, Richie Richardson, Franklyn Rose and many of the other players have told me on a few occasions that Pamela's Caribbean dishes are among some of the best food they have eaten anywhere in the world. After a Winston Davis benefit match with Lashings World XI at Campbell Park in Milton Keynes, similar comments were made by Steve Waugh, Lance Cairns and Craig Blewett. During this match, Pamela looked after their partners who were in attendance. I always remember this match because Indian cricketer, VVS Laxman and his wife are strict vegans and they only eat green salad!

Another remarkable thing happened during this particular match. Orson Nurse, who played for the Leeward Islands under-19 team and Birmingham Cavaliers, clean-bowled the great VVS Laxman for a golden duck! I was upstairs in the pavilion when this happened, and Greg Blewett and Lance Cairns kept laughing and only stopped when Laxman reached the pavilion.

During the World Cup in 2018, Rawl Lewis, the West Indies team manager, had contacted me to say they were in Southampton, and when the team arrived in Bristol he would urgently need a seamstress to cut and repair all the players' trousers as apparently they were too long. I searched and found a Caribbean dressmaker who took about three days to rectify the situation. She told me the players had about seven pairs of trousers each. Rawl Lewis paid for this service, gave me a few complimentary tickets and the players gave me some items of cricket kit for me and my daughters.

When the West Indies played at the Ageas Bowl in June 2020, they became the first team to tour England since the lockdown. As previously mentioned, I had a few texts from the players asking for Caribbean food. This was a very difficult situation and I accepted that Rawl Lewis, the manager, would not give permission. The team was in a secure 'bubble' and if one of the players had caught the virus as the result of me bringing them food, there would have been serious repercussions. I therefore arranged to go down to the Ageas Bowl in a mask and gloves and left the food at reception for the players to collect. I brought food for the twenty-five players on the first trip and then I was told that there were forty-five people in the bubble so I went

With cricketers Devon Malcolm (left) and Darren Powell at the cricket match to mark Jamaica's 50th Anniversary of Independence held at the Oval cricket ground in London in July 2012.

I was treated to lunch by former West Indies cricketer, Franklyn Rose in Ocho Rios, Jamaica, in 2014.

With West Indies cricketer Darren Sammy at the Aces Centre in Northampton in 2015.

With former West Indies cricketer, Corey
Collymore in Bristol in 2017.

With Jamaican cricketer Andre Russell at
the Triple Century Sports Bar in Kingston,
Jamaica, in 2017.

With Richie Richardson at home in
Bedford in 1994.

back with more food. It should be noted that West Indies beat England after eating my wife's food! This was not the first time that their performance improved after eating Pamela's cooking! The West Indies went on to receive the Martin Jenkins Trophy, and I contacted an official from the Cricket West Indies board and jokingly mentioned that this trophy should be shared with my wife. Several former West Indies players said they fully agreed.

Many members of past and present West Indies teams have, in turn, supported my events over the years. The money raised went back to many of the Caribbean cricketers who played league and club cricket in the UK and in the Caribbean. On one occasion I turned up at a ground in Northampton to be introduced to a young player from Barbados, and noticed that he was playing in boots with holes. I got his details and sent money for him to buy a new pair of boots. We had another cricketer from Barbados who sent me an email saying he was saving money to come to England to complete his Level 3 coaching course and that he was a hundred pounds short. I sent him the money and he said he will never forget me. I also helped another player to get his permanent stay in England.

Each April before the cricket season started I would receive a few calls from the Caribbean. I remember a cricketer from Guyana contacted me saying another cricketer gave him my number. He did not need any direct help from me but wanted to connect with someone in the UK that he could rely on in an emergency. Every summer we would receive calls from some clubs about certain Caribbean cricketers needing assistance, and we always helped by buying bats and other equipment. Franklyn Rose was very generous when he was at Northamptonshire and also for the West Indies. I remember getting lots of good quality gear from him which went to players. I also recall Marlon Samuels giving gear to a club in London as well as giving me a pair of gloves which were passed to a talented young cricketer.

GORDON GREENIDGE

I recall that Phil Simmons opened a festival in Bath for me, and Gordon Greenidge opened the Swindon Caribbean Carnival and also attended the Luton Caribbean community match. He also captained the Winston Davis XI in Milton Keynes and Bristol at the Winston Davis annual benefit match. Gordon also attended the Friends of the Caribbean Cricket Match in Milton Keynes in August 2021, along with Michael Holding, Philo Wallace and another long-time supporter of mine, Chris Lewis.

In all areas of my work, I have had the support of the former West Indies cricketer, Gordon Greenidge. Back in 1985, he attended one of the community cricket matches in Luton. Bob Baker, who was the main organiser, had wanted a West Indies player to be the special guest and Gordon agreed to attend. He also attended a community event in Northampton in 1994, along with TV soap, 'Brookside', actress Jodie Hanson.

Jimmy Adams also captained the Winston Davis match on several occasions and was one of the biggest supporters. Although he was very busy he gave up his time to come to the Victoria Mutual dinner and presentation in Bedford in 2006.

Ron Headley, who was a very good speaker, attended numerous events for me. His son, Dean Headley, attended a few events whenever he had the time. Gus Logie drove from the Central Lancashire leagues to Birmingham to play a match for the Hurricane Gilbert appeal in 1990. Nemiah Perry also travelled from the leagues to present awards to VM under-17 teams at Milton Keynes. Otis Gibson attended several VM presentations at the Centennial Centre in Birmingham, as did Desmond Haynes and Joel Garner. Before Alvin Kallicharan went to the USA, he was another regular at many of my events.

I was privileged to have Colin Croft and Ian Bishop attend Alan Warner's benefit match in Luton. Clive Lloyd, who was manager of the West Indies cricket team then, agreed that Bishop could attend as a guest but could not

History in the making: (left to right) Chair of the Victoria Mutual Caribbean Cup Competition, Steve Stephenson MBE, Courtney Walsh, Curtly Ambrose and Sir Vivian Richards. Courtney Walsh and Curtly Ambrose were honoured for 'Services to West Indies Cricket' by the Victoria Mutual Caribbean Cup Committee during the team's tour to England in 2000.

play. The deal was that I should pick up Bishop from a hotel in Gloucestershire and get him back by midnight. I was determined to get this right, so called on one of my longstanding cricket friends Ossie Lewis who did not let me down and got Bishop back to the hotel on time.

On another occasion the VM Cup committee decided to fly Courtly Ambrose from Antigua to our annual dinner and presentation in Birmingham on a Saturday night. However, Ambrose had to get back to Antigua on the Sunday. I made a deal with my friend Everett Bailey who picked up Ambrose from Gatwick airport who took him to the Albany Hotel and then on to the Centennial Centre. I agreed with Everett that he would not drink that night because he needed to get Ambrose back to the hotel by midnight, and wake up by 6 am so that he could catch the flight at Gatwick. Everett was able to carry out this task as planned. Ambrose phoned me at ten on the Sunday morning in a happy tone of voice to confirm they had got to Gatwick airport on time. He said, "Steve, when you have any more events you can count me in", as he was impressed by our professionalism.

Whilst I mainly asked West Indies players to attend these events, I also invited England players, although they were often otherwise engaged. Those that could attend included the late David Capel and his wife at our multicultural evening in Swindon. He also captained the Winston Davis XI along with David Ripley who was captain of one of the benefit matches in Milton Keynes. Derek Randall also attended a few of these events.

Amongst the tributes I have received is the following by Clayton Goodwin, journalist and author of the book *Caribbean Cricketers: From the Pioneers to Packer*.

"In my several decades as a reporter of West Indies cricket in the UK (and Caribbean); I have known Steve Stephenson as the "go to" man for help and information on every aspect of the game from club to international level. His record on promoting charity games and events, award dinners, hands-on assistance to teams and individuals, with an eye to the future and a mind on the past, is exceptional. He is the indispensable Mr West Indies Cricket UK. And that is just within my field of expertise. He has also achieved acclaim in other sports, mainly football, and in community relations and human rights for which he has been honoured with an MBE."

Over the many years, I have hosted the following notable events for West Indies cricketers: the Courtney Walsh benefit match and dinner in Birmingham in 1993; a dinner in Wellingborough, Northamptonshire, in 1994 for the WI team under the management of Wes Hall and Andy Roberts. Richie Richardson, the captain Brian Lara and Courtney

Walsh were also in attendance; under Ricky Skerritt's management, I arranged a Winston Davis luncheon in Bristol 2000 and gave two special awards for services to the game to Courtney Walsh and Curtly Ambrose; at the Café Royal in London in 2004, with the WI team under the management of Tony Howard, we honoured Shivnarine Chanderpaul and Ridley Jacobs for services to the game, and also to Brian Lara for his world record-breaking efforts; we had a reception in Bristol in 2007 for the team, under Michael Findlay, and also gave awards to several players; under the management of Omar Khan with Chris Gayle as captain, I held a reception for the team in Bristol in 2009; in May 2012, under the management of Richie Richardson and Otis Gibson as coach, I put on a special reception at the African Caribbean Centre in Northampton with the assistance of my friend Olive Robinson. We honoured Shivnarine Chanderpaul with a special plaque; under the management of Rawl Lewis and Jason Holder, we held a reception at Bristol West Indian Club in 2017.

The West Indian players gave a donation that was passed on to Winston Davis; and under the management of

With Jamaican cricketer Richard Staple at the Bahia Principe Grand hotel in Jamaica in 2014.

Rawl Lewis and Jason Holder, we held a second reception at Bristol West Indian Club in 2019.

Although I made links with the West Indies team in the 1980s, my main voluntary work started in the summer of 1993 when a Jamaican cricketer named Richard Staple was playing as a professional for March Town Cricket Club in Cambridgeshire.

This was about half an hour's drive from Bedford where I was then living. I went to watch Richard play and we then invited him home for dinner. During the visit Pamela asked him about the bad cold he had clearly caught. He replied that he was sleeping in a caravan in the field near the cricket pitch and that it was very cold. This was in September and he had three weeks left in England. As soon as he had played his last match we took him to our home where he was very happy and spent the time eating Caribbean food. When Richard returned to Jamaica he told Basil Williams ('Shot Gun Williams'), chair of the Jamaica Cricket Board, of our kindness and he personally thanked me when we met at Sabina Park. A few officials from the Jamaica Board were already aware of some of the issues players from Jamaica and other Caribbean countries had when they played professional cricket in England. For example, there was a first-class cricketer sleeping on the floor of a friend's house in London.

I was, therefore, asked to keep an eye on the Jamaican players who arrived from April to September each year. This was not difficult because being chair of the Victoria Mutual Caribbean Cup, and as VM was sponsoring two cricketers from Jamaica who played for Bristol, I was making regular visits to the leagues. Guy Reid Bailey, a member of the VM Cup committee, would also help by supporting the players who came to Bristol.

Years later I was proud to link up with Richard again when he played in England. He became captain of the United States team who played in the ICC Champions Trophy in 2005. I went to Southampton with some

Flanked by Micheal Holding, left, who was a special guest at the
Friends of the Caribbean cricket match, and Wain McIntosh, MBE,
Chair of the Friends of the Caribbean charity, in August 2021.

Caribbean food for the USA team, as Richard said they had
not eaten much Caribbean food since they had been on tour.
As Richard was the captain he had a double room so I was
able to spend the night at the hotel before the West Indies
match. During that visit Brian Lara came down the stairs
of the hotel and on seeing me with the food, asked, "Steve,
what about the West Indies?" I was surprised to see Brian,
Chris Gayle and Darren Bravo and the rest of the West
Indies team at the hotel. I was not aware that they were in
Southampton. Pamela and I then went and brought food
for the entire West Indies team as we only lived just under
an hour from the Ageas Bowl.

Richard made his first-class debut for Jamaica against
England in 1990. He played twice in the Red Stripe Cup
against the Leeward Islands and Barbados in February 1991,
and was on the West Indies tour of England later that year
playing a first-class match against a World XI at the North
Marine Road ground in Scarborough. Richard told me he
made a score of over 50 in this match. I was told a few years

later by two senior members of the West Indies team that if
he had made two decent scores in first-class cricket of 70 or
80, he would have probably got into the West Indies team.

Richard went on to play for the Progressive Cricket Club
in the New York Metropolitan Cricket League, NY Region.
He played for Jamaica in the West Indies Cricket Board
(WICB) tournaments and for the USA in the WICB Red
Stripe Bowl tournament in Jamaica, in 1997 and again in
1998/99. He also played in the International Cricket Council
(ICC) trophy tournament in Canada in 2001, and for the
US team in the 2004 ICC Six Nations Challenge in the
United Arab Emirates. He last played for the USA in the
2005 ICC Trophy in Ireland. After warm-up matches against
the Northern Cricket Union President's XI and Namibia,
he played six matches in that tournament.

In June 2020, following the arrival of the West Indies
cricket team to England, I contacted the cricket board to
suggest that the players 'take the knee' as it symbolised
the need for us to continue the fight for race equality and
justice. This was something that attracted massive support
amongst the Caribbean cricketing fraternity in the UK. The
West Indies team, led by Jason Holder, went on to 'take the
knee' with the England team at all of their matches.

MALCOLM MARSHALL

The first person I connected with in the West Indies team
was Malcolm Marshall. In 1979, the team played
Northamptonshire in a match at Simpson's ground in
Leighton Buzzard. I went to that match with my friend
Franklin Hunter and several club cricketers from Luton.
This was Malcolm's first tour and he was fielding on the
boundary and getting some 'stick' from some West Indies
fans for mis-fielding a ball. I shouted out that they should
leave the young man alone as it was his first tour. I did not
realise that 'Macca', as he came to be known, was listening.
When I returned to the ground the next day he came up to
me and said "You are back again, where are you from?"

On hearing my reply of Luton, to my surprise he confirmed that he had a brother and sister living there. It turned out that Steve Harewood, like his brother Malcolm, was a fast bowler for Chevettes, one of the West Indian clubs in Luton. Steve came from Barbados a few years earlier and was causing havoc with his short pitch bowling, especially around the local village teams in Bedfordshire.

I met Macca infrequently when he played county cricket for Hampshire. However, it was when I went to live in Birmingham that we met more often.

During the 1999 World Cup, I went to Edgbaston and brought some Caribbean food for the team. I remember the day as if it was yesterday. Arif Ali, from the *Caribbean Times* newspaper, gave me some copies of the book, *One Hundred Great West Indian Test Cricketers* that his company, Hansib Publications, had published in 1988. Armed with the last copy, I told Macca to give it to one of the players. He suggested giving it to the 'baby of the team', and on querying who that was pointed to Ramnaresh Sarwan who was making his first tour to England. I gave Sarwan the book which was gratefully received by the youngster.

I then turned to Macca and suggested that we have a drink later. He responded that he would like to but declined, pointing to the side of his back indicating what I assumed was a muscle strain. He said that he needed to rest it. I thought nothing of it because Macca had a 'whipping' bowling action, so maybe it was just a strain. Little did I know that the 'strain' turned out to be a symptom of colon cancer. About two weeks after our meeting I was told he had been admitted to the Priory Hospital in Birmingham. I tried to phone but was unable to speak to him. Malcolm Marshall passed away in Bridgetown, Barbados, on 4 November 1999 aged just 41.

I was greatly saddened to learn of his death, but I was able to pay my respects when there was a joint memorial service at Westminster Abbey in London for Malcolm

Marshall, Sylvester Clarke and Conrad Hunte. Clive Lloyd and Mickey Stewart both gave heart-warming speeches.

Conrad Hunte died of a heart attack in Sydney, Australia, on 3 December 1999, aged 67, and Sylvester Clarke became the third Test cricketer from Barbados to die in the space of five weeks when he collapsed at his home in Bridgetown on 4 December. He would have been 45 the following Saturday. These were truly sad losses to the world of cricket.

In December 2015, in a *Cricket Country* article, Abhishek Mukherjee wrote about Sylvester Clarke, the Surrey legend, who was one of the most intimidating bowlers in history. "Andy Roberts was the shrewdest of them; Michael Holding, the fastest; Joel Garner, the most accurate; Colin Croft, the most unorthodox; Malcolm Marshall, the most versatile and greatest of the pack. They were all greats of the era, combining to take West Indies to heights they had never known. But the meanest of them all? That had to be Sylvester Theophilus Clarke."

I was not surprised to read that Malcolm was top of the list! A tribute that I wrote about Malcolm Marshall was published in the *Gleaner* newspaper in 1999, as well as in a brochure for the VM annual dinner and presentation in November 1999. I was pleased to present a copy of this tribute to his wife, Connie at the the Westminster Abbey memorial service.

CLIVE LLOYD

In 1987, I began providing the West Indies cricket team with Caribbean food whenever they came to play in England. During this period, Stedman Wallen arranged several receptions for the West Indies team. When Sted realised that I was a close friend of Courtney Walsh and other players he asked me to assist him at these receptions,

In his 2015 book, *They Gave the Crowd Plenty Fun*, Colin Babb noted that: "Two years after the Windrush (1948) and the emergence of small Caribbean presence in Britain, the

With the legendary West Indies cricketer, Clive Lloyd
at the Clive Lloyd Cup Presentation in London in 1991.

West Indies cricket team beat England for the first time on
English soil at Lords. For some Caribbean migrants who
settled in Britain from the 50s onwards, the performance of
the West Indies team symbolised progress and togetherness.
West Indies victories against the England cricket team,
especially on English soil provided West Indian residents
in Britain with a source of pride and an opportunity to
witness victory against representatives of the old colonial
empire. The importance of West Indian cricket as a pan-
Caribbean force was highlighted by Clive Lloyd during his
tenure as West Indies captain."

Clive became West Indies captain in late 1974 and
within months was showing his big match temperament
with a match-winning century at Lords at the inaugural
World Cup final against Australia.

Great teams are not built overnight but sometimes a
moment, a match, or a series can be a turning point that
changes the course of history. For West Indies such a series
was their 5-1 defeat of Australia in 1975-76. They had won
the World Cup in England in 1975, but crashed back to earth
months later. They were brutalised by the menacing pace
of Dennis Lillie and Jeff Thomson, racially abused by the
crowds, and felt that they had been harshly treated by

Australian umpires. In 1989, Clive told Cyrille Regis and I that he had decided to change approach. Clive said "never again", having assessed the West Indies capabilities, and the all-out pace attack was born!

Clive retired in 1985 having administered the famous 5-0 'Blackwash' against England and a 3-1 victory against Australia. Clive was the first West Indian player to compete in 100 Tests. He led the side in 74 Tests, securing 26 without defeat and a record-breaking eleven successive victories.

I remember speaking to Arif Ali, owner of the *Caribbean Times* newspaper, who was annoyed that the great man was not given a knighthood. Fortunately, this was remedied in 2020 to the delight of me, my family and his many supporters.

Clive has continued to support West Indies cricket. He wrote to the team that made the trip to Bangladesh, telling the new players to take their chances. The West Indies came away with a 2-0 series win after both Kayle Mayer and Nkrumah Bonner took their chances. At the time of writing this book, they are now part of the West Indies first team. I remember sending a message to Clive about this initiative.

In April 2020, Clive led a scheme which brought together former Test players to help mentor cricketers around the Caribbean. This has been supported by Wavell Hinds at the West Indies Players Association (WIPA), Jimmy Adams and Marissa Aguerilla from the West Indies women's team.

THE HEADLEY FAMILY

I became chair of the Victoria Mutual Caribbean Cup national competition at the time when Courtney Walsh was president. During this period, both Ron and Dean Headley supported our events, including the Winston Davis benefit matches.

Ron Headley was a former cricketer and son of the great George Headley. He was also father of England cricketer Dean Headley. Ron and I used to go to all the Aston Villa and Coventry football matches when Cyrille Regis played for both clubs.

At the Victoria Mutual Caribbean Cup Annual Dinner and Presentation held at the Park Inn Hotel in Northampton in 2007. From left to right: my daughter, Simone, my mother, Pearl, former West Indies cricketer, Ron Headley, my daughter, Andrea, and my wife, Pamela.

I have had a long association with the Headley family, having lived on the same road as them – Mountain View Avenue in East Kingston, Jamaica. During my school days, I played cricket against Ron's brother Sydney Headley. We played 'Catchy Chubby' in a field near our home, and Sydney, who was nicknamed 'Buppy', was always difficult to dislodge from the wicket. I also played youth cricket against him when he captained Kingston College, along with Michael Holding, a terrifying fast bowler, who was also in his team.

Ron's mum Rena was one of my Sunday school teachers at Maranatha church in Deanery Road, Kingston, and his dad, whom we called Mas George or Atlas, would come to our school to coach us. I must admit that he did not coach me personally, but his assistant coach Dickie Fuller, who wore short trousers, did. Sometimes Mr Fuller would hold the back legs of players and tell them to 'play forward'. I was told that Mr Fuller played one Test for the West Indies team.

Mas George was called Atlas because he carried the burden of West Indies batting on his shoulders for many years. My uncle-in-law Lucien Hopwood told me that he not only saw George play, but served him drinks a few times when he worked in clubs and bars around Kingston. I was also told that my uncle, Tom Simpson was a good batsman who played for local clubs.

I was actually at Mas George's last cricket match and innings in Jamaica. This was at Lucas Cricket Club in Kingston when he made a duck in his benefit match and was carried off the field on the back of one of the players, O.C. Scott.

DEAN HEADLEY

In 2011, I was at Sabina Park and could not wait to see Dean make his debut against the West Indies. Ron had been talking about it long beforehand, but due to business commitments he could not make the trip. I remember the day well as the match was cancelled, due to the pitch being deemed as dangerous, after a few overs which caused an uneven bounce. Dean actually gave me fifteen tickets, some of which I gave to students on a visit to the University of the West Indies, Mona campus.

I was always proud of Dean and first saw him in the Birmingham league playing for Old Hill against Moseley. I was very impressed with his bowling and pleased when he took 7 wickets on his debut for Middlesex with 5 in one innings. I remember going to Lords when West Indies played Middlesex in a county match, and Dean took me in to the Middlesex changing room to meet Mike Gatting and the team.

Ron said that I came from the blue blood of West Indian cricket, as I think like a West Indian and played cricket like a West Indian, meaning one can't coach the talent out of us.

In 2015, I also met Ron's brother Ledlie, who was a sprinter for Jamaica at the 1964 Olympics. I was on holiday at the Bahia Principe hotel in Runaway Bay at the same time as Ron and his two daughters and he introduced us.

Ron used to tell me a lot of stories about his father and his time playing for Jamaica and county cricket. He also told me about his invention of a catalytic converter that was an anti-pollution exhaust emission system. Having been invited to a secret meeting in Stourbridge, West Midlands along with Cyrille Regis and others to discuss the system, we had to sign a non-disclosure form. Ron came to our home in Bedford once and we drove to one of the Clive Lloyd annual presentation dinners in London. Due to it being fitted with this device, the car did not burn a single gallon of petrol which was really amazing.

Although Ron told me his dad did not want him to play for the West Indies, the cricket records showed that in 1973, following an injury to Steve Camacho, Ron was co-opted from Worcestershire into the West Indies touring team. He played seven first-class matches for the West Indies, including the first and second matches of a three-match Test series. His 42 in the second innings of the first match was his highest Test score. He also played in the second of two One-Day International matches for the Prudential Trophy.

His father George Headley played 22 Tests for the West Indies, while his son Dean Headley played fifteen Tests and thirteen ODIs for England. This was the first case of three consecutive generations of the same family playing Test cricket.

Perhaps the most fitting epitaph on Headley's career came from Berkley Gaskin. When asked how he would compare the great Jamaican with the then outstanding players, headed by the three W's of Worrell, Weekes and Walcott plus Gary Sobers, he replied: "They could sit in the same cathedral as George, but not in the same pew".

Two other prominent West Indians have also commented on the significance of the great George Headley. Of Headley's meeting with the king of England in 1939, the West Indian writer Frank Birbalsingh said: "That one of us – a Black man – could shake the hand of a king introduced possibilities formerly undreamt of in our colonial backwater of racial inferiority, psychological subordination and political powerlessness."

Michael Manley, a former Jamaica prime minister and cricket writer, noted that Headley rose to success at a time of political awakening in Jamaica, when the Black majority of the population were increasingly determined to end the minority rule of landowners and challenge the racism of the time. According to Manley, the middle classes saw in Headley "the reassurance which they needed. He demonstrated Black capacity". The white upper classes were also proud of his achievements as a West Indian, but Manley writes, "it was to the Black masses that Headley had the deepest significance. He became the focus for longing of an entire people for proof: proof of their own self-worth, their own capacity. Furthermore, they wanted this proof to be laid at the door of the white man who owned the world which defined their circumstances". Manley saw the nickname of 'Atlas' not just in sporting terms, but in his carrying "the hopes of the Black, English-speaking Caribbean man ... He was Black excellence personified in a white world and in a white sport."

COURTNEY WALSH

In 1984, I first met Courtney Walsh, affectionately known as Cuddy or Mark, when Gloucestershire played Northamptonshire in a county match at Luton Town CC ground in Wardown Park. I am not sure if he acted accordingly when I suggested that he needed to be mindful of 'burn out' because Malcolm Marshall had told me the cricket management wanted him to bowl spells of 15 to 20 overs. Courtney then turned out to be the workhorse for West Indies cricket when he bowled, and I can certainly take no credit for his remarkable individual achievements of 519 Test wickets.

Courtney supported many of my charity events, and when he could not make it to a match or a reception would kindly provide cricket memorabilia. I put on a dinner and dance and cricket match at Moseley in Birmingham during his 1993 benefit year. Simon Briggs, sports writer for the

Telegraph newspaper, poignantly summed up Cuddy's remarkable achievements. "A physiological phenomenon, Courtney Walsh probably bowled faster for longer than any man in history. His spirit was as unbreakable as his body, urging him on to the previously undreamed-of heights of 519 Test wickets and 30,019 balls, not to mention the countless overs he sent down for Gloucestershire and Jamaica. For the first half of his career, Walsh was the willing workhorse cantering into the wind while Curtly Ambrose or Malcolm Marshall galloped down the hill. But he grew stronger and wilier with age, graduating to the new ball around 1993, and forming one of the great opening partnerships with Ambrose: 421 wickets between them from 49 Tests."

There have been many tributes paid to my great friend, but I will mention two in particular. Former West Indies captain Clive Lloyd said that: "I don't think you'll find another Courtney Walsh around and if I was a young fast bowler, I'd want to emulate him." And former West Indies all-rounder Gary Sobers went on to say that, "The young crop of fast bowlers can take from him his dedication to the West Indies and his ability to be always there, trying and giving 100 per cent in difficult conditions."

WINSTON DAVIS

The Winston Davis benefit match started because of a phone call from my friend and main supporter in cricket, Courtney Walsh. During the call Cuddy told me that he had been to visit Winston Davis at an orthopaedic hospital in Oswestry, Shropshire. This was a light bulb moment for me, because my eldest daughter Andrea had major surgery on one of her legs in this hospital in 1988, and spent over four weeks there. Apart from my sister-law Valerie Stephenson, Andrea did not have any other visitors. We had only lived in Birmingham for eighteen months and did not have a lot of friends in the area and as a result Pamela and I were on our own with our friend Rose, caring for her sister Simone in Sutton Coldfield.

Roy Wilkinson, Winston Davis and Ron Headley in 2002.

I contacted Winston Davis a few days after that call with the suggestion of starting an annual benefit match. Winston was very surprised by my offer, since we had never met and it was the first time we had spoken to each other. However, any friend of Cuddy could be a friend of mine.

Matthew Engel, a writer for *The Guardian* newspaper and editor of *Wisden* reflected upon Winston Davis following the tragic accident in 1997 which left him paralysed from the neck down:

"He played 15 Tests for the West Indies; he held the record for the best bowling figures in the history of the World Cup – seven for 51 against Australia on an old fashioned dodgy Headingly pitch in 1983; and he had a reputation as one of the nicest guys in the game.

Had he been born in any other country or any other era apart from the one that produced Michael Holding, Andy Roberts and Joel Garner, Winston would probably have played 100 Tests. But in the mighty West Indies team of the 1980s he was a reserve more often than not.

... Even before the accident, his Christian faith was the most important thing in his life. If anything, disaster reinforced this. He would talk about the ways it had changed his life for the better, about the wonderful people he had met as a result, about how lucky he was that his mind was unaffected. ... Above all, Winston wants to give rather than to receive. And he can give us a great deal, because his response to adversity is a potential inspiration to all of us ... He is an exceptional man."

One of my events was a luncheon for Winston in the presence of the full West Indies team, captained by Brian Lara. This event took place at the Bristol West Indies cricket club and coincided with me working on the book *Cold Arrival: Life in a Second Homeland* at the African Caribbean Centre. I asked my friend Olive Robinson if she could organise a coach trip for the elders to meet the West Indies team. Olive obliged, and we took a full coach load to Bristol. My wife Pamela did the catering. She was not only praised by Ricky Skerritt, the manager of the West Indies team, and the players, but was paid a big compliment by the elders who all enjoyed their meals. I recall Mr Douglas, the oldest member of the club, commenting on the excellent Caribbean meal he had eaten and he has had many in his time at the club and in the Caribbean.

VIV RICHARDS

From the first time I met Vivian Richards and he found out about the work I have been actively doing within our community he always supported me. I believe it was my friend Novel James, affectionately known as Huggins, who 'big me up' to Viv. He was always in demand and very busy, but whenever we met up he always found time for me.

During Viv's captaincy in 1988 I brought food for the players on a regular basis and had access to the players' changing room. I can't remember exactly who, but either

Pictured with my daughter, Simone, and the West Indies cricket legend, Sir Vivian Richards at the Glamorgan v Sussex cricket match in Brighton in 1991.

Viv or Courtney told me everything there was confidential and I had to leave the room about five minutes before the interval, but could return later to collect autographs, bats etc. From that point onwards I also respected this unwritten protocol, and to this day I have never mentioned to anyone anything that I had seen or heard. The dressing room was like any other cricket club, except it was the great West Indies team, with great players in a very small space. In 1988 I raised several hundred pounds from the cricket memorabilia, and I was able to help several cricketers from the Caribbean with cricket gear and give some additional financial help.

Viv brought a lot of joy to us as a batsman. According to Sir Hilary Beckles, cricket author and Vice Chancellor of the University of the West Indies, English players on the opposing team were thrown into panic when they faced Viv Richards. They sensed that for the Antiguan, cricket was for the business of history and politics and the struggle for justice and inequality

For Richards competing against England was more than just a competitive game of international cricket. It was an opportunity to assert himself and his colleagues as a collective Caribbean force. In this way cricket was viewed as one of the few arenas that the Black person from the Caribbean could compete with a white person on the basis of equality.

Colin Babb stated: "Viv Richards was more than willing to express an understanding of the West Indian migrants' social condition and daily struggles in Britain. As captain of the West Indies 1988 tour of England, Richards outlined the responsibility of representing the Caribbean community living in Britain. He considered that it was important for him to perform for West Indians in Britain who don't have too great a life".

In one match between Glamorgan and Sussex at Hove, Viv had left tickets from me and his long-time friend Joseph from Luton. We arrived at the gate along with my daughter Simone about two hours late for the match and were told there were no tickets. We contacted Viv who I always called the 'Master' and he came down to the gate and demanded that they hand over the tickets. The steward on the gate was quite surprised, and they then let us in to the ground with tickets for the members' area. A fan came over to Viv and tried to barge his way into our conversation. Viv told him in a no nonsense manner to wait, because his friends whom he had not seen for a long time had travelled a long way to see him.

Viv paid me a massive tribute when he came to Bristol along with Sted Wallen for a Channel 4 television programme. On arrival the 'Master' gave me a big hug instead of shaking my hand, as he did with some of his fans. During his speech, he told the crowd that on many occasions I had supported the team when he was playing by bringing them Caribbean food which was well appreciated. Viv then went on to thank me for continuing to support the West Indies team.

Viv also visited our home in Bedford, along with Steve Bastein and Darrell Foster, the three Black players that were then in the Somerset team. He went on to captain the Winston Davis Team at Campbell Park, Milton Keynes and drew a larger than average crowd on a cold day.

CHRIS GAYLE

I had a good relationship with Chris before he became famous as I remember him coming to play for Worcestershire in 2005. After phoning him, I went to his penthouse flat with a week's supply of Caribbean food which he appreciated very much. He was then leaving for Australia and needed to stay in London overnight. I contacted the Jamaican High Commission who sorted out a hotel for him. He had to get a visa to go to Australia so I told him that when he goes to the Australian embassy in the Strand he should not have any problems once they realise he is a professional cricketer. He later phoned to say he got his visa and was on his way to Australia.

West Indies cricketer, Chris Gayle honoured me for my support by presenting me with a signed cricket bat in 2015.

West Indies cricketer, Chris Gayle presenting me with a
signed team shirt for 'Services to West Indies Cricket' at
Bristol West Indian Phoenix CC in May 2019.

He once had some issues with the West Indies Board,
so we met in the gardens at Pegasus hotel in Kingston for a
confidential chat, near to the tennis court. Coincidentally,
Kevin Riley who played for Lucas CC with Chris was the
tennis coach at the Pegasus, and I had helped him when he
played league cricket in England, including getting him a
contract to play for Moseley in the Birmingham league.

It was interesting to note that a lot of people were
staring at us in the Pegasus Hotel, but we did not think
anything of it. However, whilst walking back a gentleman
jumped out of the swimming pool and asked if that was
Chris Gayle to which I responded "Yes". He wanted to take
a photo with Chris who willingly agreed. The man
mentioned being a pilot for Virgin Atlantic, and I said that
airline had brought me to Jamaica. He then surprisingly
said that he will secure me a first-class seat on my return
flight to the UK. I did not think much about the offer,
because in the past people had made promises and never
keep them. However, as soon as I sat down on the plane my

name was called and I returned to England travelling first-class, seated beside an English actress. I told Chris the story and he had a big smile on his face.

I am pleased to say that Pamela and I saw one of Chris's greatest innings when he played for Somerset in a Twenty-Twenty game in 2015. Chris made a spectacular unbeaten 124 not out. He hit a ball in to the river behind the grounds, and a fan retrieved it as souvenir which Chris duly signed and had a drink with him. I was really impressed that after the match there was a long line of fans about 150 yards in length waiting in front of the pavilion, and Chris stood there signing autographs and taking photos with everyone. I told him afterwards just how proud Pamela and I were of him as there were only a few Caribbean people in the grounds. At another match he came straight over with the 'Man of the Match' champagne and asked me to give it to Pamela, adding how he really appreciated her Caribbean food.

During the 2018 World Cup my daughter Simone wanted to go the Ageas Bowl to see the West Indies, but the weather in September was a bit too cold for her due to her on-going cancer treatment. I told Chris who arranged for two VIP tickets with a champagne breakfast for myself and Simone. We really appreciated this because she could sit in the warmth to watch the match. Since the early days Chris has remained the same, despite the fact that he holds many records.

Here are just a few: He was the first player to hit a six with the first ball of a Test match. He was the first batsman in the world to score three centuries in all formats of the game, and one of only four players, Don Bradman, Brain Lara and Vireneder Sewagh, to score two triple centuries in Test cricket.

A lot of people have asked me about the tribute that Chris gave me in Bristol in May 2019. This is what he said:

"There are many great people in West Indies cricket and here tonight we are with one of them. Thanks,

Mr Steve Stephenson. We know of the great cricketers who play on the field, but the world doesn't always get to see some of the great people who make their contribution off the field. We want to again thank Steve for what he has done and will continue to do for the cricketers, the game of cricket and the people of the West Indies."

CHAPTER NINE

Concluding Thoughts

For the past forty years I have been employed as a social worker and an equality officer in local government and with community groups. During this time I worked in the heart of deprived communities like Handsworth in Birmingham, and St Pauls in Bristol. These two disciplines are some of the most demanding and challenging jobs in this country.

At different times it feels like race equality appears to be at a standstill in the UK. Inequality, lack of social mobility and exclusion from the economic, social, cultural and political spheres are among the key challenges facing the UK's Black, Asian and Minority Ethnic communities. Such exclusion and inequality, whether it is driven by race, class, gender or any of the other means of dividing the country, have a huge cost.

The Race and Ethnic Disparity Commission, to which I made a submission, have now compounded the issue by playing down the term 'institutional racism' and the despicable role of the slave trade. In *The Guardian* newspaper, the historian, writer and broadcaster, David Olusoga wrote: "shockingly the authors – perhaps unwittingly – deploy a version of an argument that was used by the slave owners themselves in the defence of slavery 200 years ago: the idea that becoming culturally British, Black people were somehow beneficiaries of the system."

Many people were disheartened by the findings of the Commission's report. Whilst things might have improved in recent decades the lived experience of Black and Asian people does not bear this out. "Who feels it, knows it," has to be reiterated. Experiences of racial discrimination are real and there should be no attempt to gaslight the issues with generalised and selective statistics. After many false dawns and promises will 2021 be the year when our voices are finally heard, despite this blinkered and narrow-minded report?

Fredrick Douglas, the great abolitionist agitator once said, "Find out just what any people will quietly submit to and you have the exact measure of the injustice and wrong which will be imposed on them."

The Covid-19 pandemic has further highlighted some of the many injustices that Black, Asian and minority ethnic people face on a daily basis. A report in May 2020 by the University of Manchester's Centre on Dynamics of Ethnicity (CoDE) highlighted the extent of the UK's race inequality, with Covid-19 likely to worsen the problem.

CoDE is a four year interdisciplinary programme of research concerned with understanding changing ethnic inequalities and identities. This major new study has found that systemic and persistent racial inequalities in employment, health, housing and education, continue to blight the lives of ethnic minority people in the UK – and worryingly this puts them at greater risk from the impact of the Covid-19 crisis. For example, ethnic minorities are already more likely to be in low-paid, insecure work, more likely to suffer ill-health and more likely to live in overcrowded conditions, even before the outbreak.

"Over 50 years after race relations legislation was passed, ethnic minorities in Britain continue to experience extensive inequalities in areas such as education, employment, housing and health", said Dr Omar Khan, director of the Runnymede Trust. "Even before Covid-19 there was too little action to tackle these inequalities, while there are now concerns that the pandemic and Britain's response to it will instead worsen historic and systemic racial inequalities."

In addition, the Office of National Statistics (ONS) clearly shows that some occupations have a higher risk level for Covid-19 which is linked by an over representation of BAME community members. The ONS emphasise that assembly workers, care workers, home carers and retail assistants have the highest risk of dying. Among men, factory workers, security guards, chefs, restaurant workers, taxi and bus drivers are most at risk. The figures also reveal that nurses are twice as likely to die as their peers. Whilst working as a social worker a Muslim man once told me that men from his community were attracted to driving taxis because they don't drink alcohol, therefore the weekend trade is very good for these men picking up people who are out on the town. As a result, they are now at a much greater level of risk.

These inequalities have been compounded by a disproportionately large number from the BAME communities being very suspicious about having the vaccine. This has highlighted their mistrust and lack of confidence in the NHS and other institutions due to their 'lived experience' of all forms of discrimination.

The Race Relations Amendment Act of 2000 was a chance to fundamentally address racism in Britain, but in reality little has changed. This Act was one of our most progressive pieces of anti-racist legislation, but over the past 20 years it has proved to be the most weakly enforced law on the statute books. Some commentators argue that the Act has failed which is a bit misleading as how can legislation fail on its own, when those who were meant to implement it do not take ownership?

I had direct experience of this whilst working as an equality officer. What some people do not understand is that there were, and still are, a lot of double-standards when it comes to race. The same officers in public sector bodies who failed to implement the Act would quote and implement other legislation on a daily basis, whilst race was still a taboo subject to many of them.

The Act itself was a direct response to the Macpherson report of 1999 which found that the police force was institutionally racist following the Met's gross mishandling of the Stephen Lawrence case. The Act built on previous legislation and was seen as progressive because it places a legal duty on public institutions to promote race equality (including the government), and to proactively ensure that major initiatives do not negatively affect racial equality.

The way to do this was to implement race equality impact assessments which must be carried out before institutions make significant changes. Together with the strong wording of the Macpherson report there was hope that New Labour would seriously tackle institutional racism while in office. There was hope that the year 2000 would mark a turning point in addressing racism in Britain.

Over the past 20 years those hopes have been dashed. The major target of the reforms, the police force, is as institutionally racist today as it was in 2000. Disproportionate rates of stop-and-search continue to blight both the force and the Black youths who are mostly subject to them, to the extent that many of the worst-offending services tried to stop collecting data on ethnicity during such stops.

Meanwhile, the largest public sector body, the NHS, recently launched its own workforce equality standard in recognition of the entrenched and systematic discrimination it still operates in terms of employment. In fact, across all public institutions it is evident that little has changed in the last 20 years.

Not only is the Race Relations (Amendment) Act completely ineffectual, it has now become an active device for institutions to cover their discriminatory tracks. A few of my colleagues who are still working in the race and equality field feel that rather than challenge racial inequality the law has become a fig leaf for further discrimination.

The Equality Act of 2010 was supposed to provide a modern, single, legal framework with a clear law to better tackle disadvantage and discrimination.

Whilst advocating for social justice and racial equality for our community, as a social worker by profession I always showed humanity to everyone, irrespective of their ethnicity. I know that 'white lives matter' as well, and am fully aware of poor white families with individuals who under the protected characteristics in the Equality Act 2010 are vulnerable. However, we still need to have an honest conversation around race, which remains a taboo subject.

Lord Simon Wooley who set up Operation Black Vote in 1996 was made chair of the government's Race Disparity Unit in 2018. He said sadly that this government has set itself against the greatest conversation our nation still needs to have. However, he hopes signs of unity from last summer "when millions of Black and white protesters took to the streets" bode well for the future. I fully agree with his sentiments.

On 25 May 2021, it was the first anniversary of George Floyd's death. Writing in the *Daily Mirror* Darren Lewis commented that, "… only on the surface has anything at all changed since May 25 last year when George Floyd was killed. Visibility has improved across a range of organisations. The dial however, has simply moved from minus-five to zero. Many of our white allies who are actively fighting for change inside the arts, education, sports, industry and the media, now understand why Black people are exhausted … the only real cause for optimism is that there are more white people prepared to highlight the issues."

TAKING THE KNEE

The 'Taking of the Knee' was no doubt a powerful gesture at the beginning, but we need to see action and meaningful change. Some individuals and institutions are now talking in a politically correct way, but I also heard this after the 1981 and 1985 uprisings, and after the Macpherson report following the death of Stephen Lawrence, but there have only been incremental changes. The Black Lives Matter movement does appear to have more momentum, at least for now.

However, some Tory members of Parliament have spoken out against 'taking the knee' in football, after England fans booed the players in two friendly matches before the Euros in June 2020. They also criticised the ECB for taking action against cricketer Ollie Robinson after his sexist and racist tweets. Some ministers still refuse to complete Equality training, and on top of that we have the Home Office's despicable treatment of the Windrush victims. Are we really making any progress?

Looking more broadly, addressing institutional discrimination and inequalities associated with race and other protected characteristics takes commitment, evidence, leadership, legislative tools, a long term vision, support and time. There is always scope for improvement in the Public Sector Equality Duty's (PSED) requirements, and in its practical application. The most important factor in ensuring the most effective implementation of the PSED is leadership from senior management and political leaders alike to provide equality and justice for all.

BLACK LIVES MATTER

The BLM protests have at least forced people to begin to have those difficult discussions about race, class, poverty and attainment.

In my national profile on the Operation Black Vote website I made the following comments, "Britain is now more diverse - ethnically, racially and culturally. Diversity has brought benefits. But change and migration have also brought challenges. And so clarifying how we promote, challenge and deliver race, equality and human rights are more vital than ever." Some people like me have been fighting these issues long before 'Black Lives Matter', and will continue to do so, long after the marches stop. Many of the young people on the marches, both Black and white, need to learn the lessons from the past.

Currently, young Black people are significantly overrepresented in the criminal justice system in the UK, and when they enter that system their life chances are significantly damaged. According to the Lammy Review in 2017 – an independent survey of the treatment of Black, Asian and minority ethnic individuals in the criminal justice system as a whole – youngsters from these backgrounds made up 45 per cent of the custodial population, despite only comprising 18 per cent of the 10-17 year old population. They also accounted for 28 per cent of the children arrested, and 25 per cent of the total children who received a caution or conviction, a seven per cent increase compared to ten years ago.

A parallel to the socio-economic deprivation experienced by Black Caribbean boys is that of white working-class boys. Speaking with my social worker's hat on, I have worked with many vulnerable white boys. Currently, around 10 per cent of white pupils, 20 per cent of Black pupils and 45 per cent of Bangladeshi pupils receive free school meals. In total, there were 33,697 boys on free school meals who sat their GCSEs in 2019. Of these, 1,093 Bangladeshi boys achieved an average score of 42.8; 2,880 Black boys achieved an average score of 34.5; and 22,720 white boys achieved an average score of 28.5.

The data shows us that the white boys in receipt of free school meals are falling behind, but it also highlights the fact that there are a huge number of disadvantaged pupils in the system that need support to unlock their potential.

ROLE MODELS

There is always a need to be aware of the role models that we present to children through play equipment. If all the images of Black people presented to children are the same as the stereotypical images shown on television, then children are going to believe that Black people can only pursue certain careers. This limits the career growth of Black children.

Unless specific steps are taken to intervene and counter this process, white children will continue to develop a sense of superiority over Black children because their choices are so wide, varied and stimulating. (i.e. *He Man, Master of the Universe* and many others are always depicted as white)

IMAGES ON PACKAGING

The packaging of play equipment is as important as the toys themselves. Black children are not often seen on the boxes of toys, nappies or any other baby products, although there is some evidence that this is changing. This again reinforces the idea that white skin, blue eyes and blonde hair are the accepted ideal.

Manufacturers have a vital role to play. As the providers of resources, it is essential that they realise their special responsibility to all children within our communities.

In the development of a child's identity positive images of people, situations and events which are recognisably part of the child's history and way of life must be offered, to ensure that they are able to value and respect themselves, whilst believing others to be their equal. We use resources with young children to stimulate and monitor their development and to help lay the foundation for formal education later on. These resources can be used to help provide a sense of identity, role models and positive images in particular for Black children.

MULTI-CULTURAL PLAY

True multi-cultural play can only occur in a society that is free from racism. This is not the case at present. We live in a society which is made up of people from many different cultures, but in which a different value is placed on each culture, white Anglo-Saxon being the most highly valued. We must begin to take positive action to counterbalance the harm that is continually being done to all children, but especially those from the less-valued cultures, namely Black children. We need to take a positive stand against racism through play, valuing all cultures equally through the resources used with young children.

One's identity is like the foundations of a building; if you don't have solid foundations, you won't have a stable building.

WHITE PRIVILEGE

As a minority group, we people of colour still need to redress the imbalances that exist in Britain today. We still don't have the same level of privilege as white people, even though some commentators would argue that disadvantaged white people such as the pupils discussed above, also don't have 'white privilege'.

This phrase 'white privilege' was first coined by activist and scholar Peggy McIntosh in 1988. She described 'white privilege' in terms of the unspoken advantage that the dominant culture has over people of colour. In other words, power, benefits and other advantages are distributed in unequal ways among the different groups in society. Specifically, with respect to white privilege, the advantage necessarily rests with white people.

'White privilege' is a far-reaching concept that highlights the unfair societal advantages that white people have over non-white people. It is something that is pervasive throughout society, and exists in all of the major systems and institutions that operate in society, as well as on an interpersonal level. If you are a white person and feel that the concept of 'white privilege' doesn't pertain to you, you are most likely mistaken. 'White privilege' is an advantage that protects white people against any form of discrimination related to their ethnicity and race, whether they are aware of it or not.

'White privilege', however, does not imply that white people have not or cannot experience challenges in life, it simply means that any challenges that a white person has faced or may face are not related to the colour of their skin. As a social worker by profession I fully understand that many white people are disadvantaged, and may not agree wholeheartedly with this concept, but undoubtedly matters are further compounded when you are Black.

The term has a long history, but it has come into sharper focus due to recent events such as the murder of George Floyd and the resulting 'Black Lives Matter' protests.

There are numerous examples of a Black person driving around in a wealthy, predominantly white neighbourhood, in an expensive car, who has been stopped by the police simply because of the colour of their skin. As a white person, do you fear that you may be pulled over for questioning by the police because your skin colour is deemed as threatening or out of place? It is highly unlikely that this fear will apply to you.

With regards to my personal experience, I was once followed around a shop in Luton and after being unable to find the item I wanted to purchase, asked the white shop assistant, "Why are you following me?" She took a step back and said that there has been a lot of shop-lifting! So the negative racial stereotype was clearly on display with me as a Black man being a potential shoplifter.

I have also noted a big difference in reactions depending on the way I was dressed. I always take pride in my appearance and wear a suit and tie to work every day. However at weekends and holidays I wear a tracksuit or cricket top and bottoms. When I am in a suit and tie, people appear to be more welcoming and courteous. When I am in casual clothes I note that some people will 'talk down to me' in shops and banks, especially when they hear my Jamaican accent which is something I am very proud of. There is a sub-conscious bias and stereotype that people will not admit to, as with an accent you are deemed to be different and seen as less educated. Many of my Black colleagues have shared similar experiences.

RACISM AND THE ENGLISH LANGUAGE

The English language has many negative meanings for the word 'black', including evil, bad and wicked. The word white has lots of positive meanings and very few negative ones. (*Roget's Thesaurus* has 88 connotations of 'black' in a bad light.) We all know that a little white lie is quite harmless, but a black lie is totally wicked and must be punished. (In the television soap, EastEnders, the character Angie once said, "I told dirty Den a little white lie but it was actually a big black lie.")

More evidence of the imbalance of the English language can be seen in children's stories and rhymes. Take for instance the ugly brown duckling, rejected by all, until he becomes a beautiful white swan, or the blonde princess in a tower waiting for the handsome white knight to come along, or how often the beast in 'Beauty and the Beast' is black, rather than white.

It is no wonder that Black children can begin to feel that, "being Black is hard work", as a young child was heard to tell his mum.

ACCEPTANCE AND PERCEPTIONS

I have had many situations in both my work and my social life where I have been more or less been invisible in some people's eyes, until they find out about my background. In one of my jobs I used to walk along a corridor every day and apart me saying good morning and some people replying, it was only an Asian cleaner that spoke to me on a regular basis. One Monday morning my manager asked me how was my weekend? I said that I went to see my friend Mark Walters playing a football match for Liverpool Football Club. After the match Mark and I were taken out by John Barnes and I also met Mick, the actor from the TV soap, Brookside. My manager was greatly surprised to hear that I and John Barnes were virtually neighbours in Kingston where we were born, although I did not know him in Jamaica. John lived in Up Park Camp with his family and I lived just outside the camp.

The word then got around that I was a friend of John and Mark who both play for Liverpool and England. They were also told that I had an MBE from the Queen. All of a sudden everyone was talking to me and wanting to know if

I could get tickets for matches. I did not really appreciate this because I am a man and human being first, regardless of status and who are my friends. I had been ignored by most people until they found out that I knew some famous people, and that I had met the Queen at Buckingham Palace.

I experienced a similar situation at a Private Members Club. Pamela and I were ignored by most people until I received a Special Award for Sports during Jamaica's 50th Anniversary of Independence celebrations in August 2012, which was reported in the local newspaper. I went back to the club on the Saturday after the report came out and a gentleman with a very posh accent invited me to sit at his table anytime. He told me that he was impressed with the story in the paper, and the fact that I received an MBE form the Queen in 1996. I was no longer invisible in his and other people's eyes.

BEING ANTI-RACIST DOES NOT MEAN BEING ANTI-WHITE

Despite these ongoing issues, I have always shown my humanity to all people. I would like to illustrate this with the following example: During a cricket tour to Jamaica in 1994, with players from London and Bristol West Indian Cricket club, my friend Guy Reid Bailey who was on the VM Cricket Committee asked me to get two tickets at Sabina Park for two of his white English friends. I sorted out the tickets and took them to their seats in the George Headley Stand. Later during the day, I met some English people from the Midlands. One couple came in from their hotel on the north coast and were struggling to find a hotel in Kingston. Someone was trying to send them to a hotel past Stoney Hill, but they were also looking for a night out, after the Test match. I told them that if they went so far out of Kingston, it would be difficult to get a taxi late at night to take them back. I was able to point them to a hotel not too far from New Kingston, were most of the Night Clubs were located.

One of the c⌐
the day, and whe
me. "Mr Stephe1
justice in Engla⌐
helping these En
him that "being
white". He looked
thought of that.

Another perso
whom I am very ¡
personal trainer fr⌐
for peaceful protest ⌐
carrying an injured, ⌐
a Black Lives Matte⌐
However, it has
This is why I have
inequality. I will cor
is fully integrated a⌐
are a thing of the pa
that struggle has to

⌐ generosity during
⌐ evening he said to
⌐ht for equality and
v why are you are
⌐d to him and told
⌐t mean being anti-
⌐at he had not really

⌐ved his humanity and
⌐ick Hutchinson. The
⌐e a powerful symbol
⌐ he was photographed
⌐testor to safety during
in London.
⌐ift people's attitudes.
⌐hallenge all forms of
⌐e cause' until Britain
⌐r forms of inequality
⌐be in my lifetime, but

THE FOUR BLACK MP⌐

I must mention a mos⌐
moment in the histor⌐
Election of 1987, whi⌐
House of Commons of
All were Labour Party
⌐essive and watershed
⌐ngdom: the General
⌐ric elevation to the
⌐mbers of parliament.
Abbott, Paul Boateng,
Bernie Grant and Keith Vaz. They joined the Black Labour
peer Lord David Pitt, who had been appointed to the House
of Lords in 1975. This was a very proud moment for me,
my friends and colleagues, who have been involved in the
fight for race equality, human rights and justice for many
years.

While I have met all four MPs over the years at various
events and occasions, I don't claim to be a personal friend
to any of them, but I am honoured to have been in their
presence.

BERNIE GRANT

I had a connection with Bernie Grant through the lady who became his wife. Sharon Grant née Lawrence was my social policy lecturer during my social work course at Hatfield Polytechnic. She was an excellent lecturer and supported the African Caribbean Society at the polytechnic. She later went on to become Bernie's personal assistant.

In 1993, I attended the launch of the *Ethnic Minorities Directory*, published by Hansib Publications, and hosted by the publisher Arif Ali at the House of Commons. It was at this event that Bernie introduced me to Tony Blair, who became the Leader of the Labour Party the following year and who would later become Prime Minister in 1997.

I was on Channel Four Television in Bernie's presence in 1987 during an election special debate with the presenters Trevor Phillips and Beverley Anderson. I was a member of the audience and spoke briefly about the plight of Black youths in British society, which went down well with the young people in Luton with whom I was working.

In the political sphere, Bernie Grant joined the Labour Party in 1975 and was elected as Member of Parliament for Tottenham, in north London, in June 1987. He brought to parliament a long and distinguished record as a leading campaigner against injustice and racism.

Bernie had served for a decade as a local councillor in the London Borough of Haringey of which he was elected leader in 1985. He was the first Black leader of a local authority in Europe who, in this capacity, had responsibility for an annual budget of some £500 million and the well-being of a quarter of a million people, many of whom were Black and ethnic minorities. He was generally regarded as the authentic voice of Britain's ethnic minorities.

When I started teaching Black studies at the Starlight Youth Club nearly all our heroes were Black Americans due their prominence in the United States. However, because of people like Bernie Grant we no longer have to look to that country for our heroes and heroines, as we now have many of our very own.

Bernie was a much loved member of the Black community and a dedicated Member of Parliament. He passed away on 8 April 2000.

DIANE ABBOTT

Diane Abbott's election victory to represent the London constituency of Hackney North and Stoke Newington made her Britain's first Black female MP. Since then, Diane has achieved so much, including setting up the London Schools and the Black Child (LSBC) initiative to challenge and raise awareness of how the British education system fails Black children.

I met Diane for the first time when she came to speak at a seminar at the Luton West Indian Community Association in 1992. She was accompanied by Pola Uddin (now Baroness Uddin), who was the first Muslim and second Asian woman to sit in Parliament.

When I received a special award for sports at the 50th anniversary celebrations at Arsenal's Emirates Stadium in London, Diane Abbott was one of the first people to congratulate me.

PAUL BOATENG

Paul Boateng was elected as the Labour MP for Brent South in 1987, and in 1988, he became Opposition spokesman on Treasury and Economic Affairs. His appointment as Chief Secretary to the Treasury marked a political hat-trick for the Brent South MP, who was also the UK's first Black government minister and first British-born Black Privy Council member. This was welcomed by race campaigners who had urged Tony Blair to promote ethnic minority talent.

I met Paul before he became an MP at an exhibition of Black sportsmen at Luton's Central Library in 1982. This event featured the likes of Henry Rhiney, the former

European welterweight boxing champion. Paul was the special guest and we were introduced to each other before his speech. Later that year our paths crossed again when he spoke at a probation seminar whilst I was a student on a probation placement. I sat with him and Trevor Hall, who was the director of Rugby Community Relations Council.

KEITH VAZ

I first met Keith Vaz in my role as principal officer of ethnic minorities for Northamptonshire County Council in 1992 when he spoke at an event in Wellingborough. We met again at Lords Cricket Club at an event to honour Sonny Ramadhin and Alf Valentine, the two great West Indian spin bowlers. In those days mobile phones were uncommon, but I had a fairly large car phone as part of my job. Keith asked for the use of my phone to make a call to the House of Commons and I willingly obliged. Later, whilst telling my manager, Ian Winter, he smiled and jokingly asked Keith had paid the bill!

A commentator said that his gaining a parliamentary seat for Leicester East from the Conservative Party would have been a remarkable achievement in any year, but coming as it did in June 1987, when the national trend was overwhelmingly in the other direction, his arrival as a Black Member of Parliament was viewed as a major political feat. At the age of 32, he was Labour's youngest MP.

LORD OUSELEY

At the time of going to press, Hansib Publications published Herman Ouseley's autobiography entitled *Belonging: Fate and Changing Realities*. I have no doubt that this book will add to the debate about equality and justice. I would like to honour Lord Ouseley whom I and my colleagues in the equality field owe a great debt of gratitude. He is not only the founder of the anti-racism and anti-discrimination organisation Kick It Out, but he has also been at the forefront of challenging institutional racism and an advocate for people from disadvantaged and deprived backgrounds for nearly sixty years.

Throughout his years in local government, heading the London Borough of Lambeth, the Inner London Education Authority and the Commission for Racial Equality, he has been a shining and guiding light for our community.

MARVIN REES BRISTOL

In May 2021, my old friend Marvin Rees was re-elected as Mayor of Bristol along with Asher Craig as Deputy Mayor. If he sets his sights on national government, I feel that he has the makings of an excellent Member of Parliament.

STEPHEN LAWRENCE

In 1998, and whilst director of Milton Keynes Race Equality Council, I attended the Stephen Lawrence Inquiry in Birmingham. I met Sir William Macpherson and two of his three advisors: Dr Richard Stone and the Right Reverend Dr John Sentamu. The atmosphere was very tense, with the Black community sitting on one side of the hall and the police on the other. My colleague, Maxie Hayles, who has long been in the struggle for race equality and human rights, had invited Sir William to Birmingham. He was one of the panel members who questioned the directors in the various departments of the council.

I remember the day quite well as it was like a war zone in the building, with community leaders understandably getting quite angry by the trivial, insensitive and patronising responses that were being given by the senior officers. Stephen Lawrence's father, Neville Lawrence, broke down and I, along with some others, went to comfort him. Later, through my connection with Bob Baker, I was invited by Bedfordshire police to run a training course on the lessons learnt from the Macpherson Report. There were thirty young policemen in the room and their body language showed that some did not want to be there. However, unlike my other colleagues who made presentations in other parts of the country, at least they were not rude or aggressive to me. Nevertheless, they clearly found it difficult to accept that their police force was institutionally racist.

SUBMISSION TO THE GOVERNMENT RACE DISPARITIES COMMISSION

On 30 November 2020, I made a submission on behalf of the Jamaican Diaspora UK (JDUK) to the Government Race Disparities Commission, chaired by Tony Sewell. I was part of a group of four people from JDUK's national board, with the others being Dr Kevin Brown (chair), Elizabeth Mullings-Smith and Fitzroy Grant. There are 23 members on the national board, but none of us were invited to sit on the commission as Boris Johnson, Britain's prime minister, cherry-picked who would best suit his agenda and play to his tune.

My submission called for all public bodies to review their equality policies with special regard to race. This needed to start with the 70 recommendations from the Macpherson report which were never really implemented. The definition of institutional racism still remains relevant today. Unfortunately, in my time in local government, there was a culture of resistance to the definition, despite evidence from numerous reports that it exists.

Instead of building on the recommendations from the Macpherson report, the Race Disparity Commission chose to try and change the narrative, despite evidence that showed that there have only been incremental changes in the UK. The UK is not yet a post-racial society, and personal experiences of prejudice and discrimination still exist, along with outright racism. So why it is that institutional racism was dismissed when it is caused by individuals and institutions amounting to a collective failure on their part to take into account, colour, culture and ethnic origin and thus disadvantaging Black, Asian and minority ethnic people?

I asked the commission just how many times we needed to repeat the same evidence that illustrated how little had really changed. The 2011 census showed that the Caribbean community are 1.1 per cent of the population, but are disproportionally represented in most areas of public life. Clearly nowhere near enough progress has been made, despite the Windrush scandal and our countless contributions to British society over the past fifty years.

As far as education was concerned, my submission to the commission said that all schools needed to add Black history to the curriculum, if they had not already done so. Furthermore, all teachers and staff in schools needed compulsory race and equality training to look at their attitude and behaviour.

THE RACE COMMISSION'S REPORT

I agree with the headline published on 1 April 2021 in the *Daily Mirror* which summed up the Report stating: 'Race Report is an insult'. However, the article went on to say that, "Today's generation of Black Britons and British Asians face less prejudice than their parents' generation." Whilst that may be partially true, this was no reason to rest on one's laurels or to pretend that racism does not continue to exist here. That is why the Race Commission Report has done Black and Asian communities a disservice.

Overall, the Commission appeared more intent on provoking a row than seeking to tackle hatred and discrimination. Its claim there is no evidence of institutional racism flies in the face of polling by *Hope Not Hate,* which found that 45 per cent of Black Britons and British Asians have experienced or witnessed racial abuse in the last twelve months, and 54 per cent think Britain is institutionally racist.

The Commission needs to explain how it reached such a conclusion, when the figures show that Black Britons are excluded from the higher ranks of almost every major profession, and that people from ethnic minority backgrounds are twice as likely to be unemployed and twice as likely to die from Covid-19. This was a chance to set out a clear path in that task of tackling ingrained inequality and injustice. The Report failed to do so, and insulted the very people it was meant to throw a lifeline and glimmer of hope to.

Baroness Doreen Lawrence, the mother of Stephen Lawrence, stated that the Report "risks giving a green light to racists". She added that her son was murdered because of racism which is something that one simply cannot forget, and that the authors of the Report are out of touch with reality. She was truly dismayed to discover that the Report claimed there was no evidence of institutional racism in Britain!!

The report was branded as "insulting and divisive" by critics. and triggered an outcry for appearing to put a positive spin on the legacy of slavery. It is noted that Boris Johnson's most senior Black advisor, Samuel Kasumu, decided to step down from his role in May although Number 10 was eager to point out that was not a link to the Report as he had threatened to quit in February. The prime minister did, however, admit that there were serious issues that our society faced to do with racism.

The National Black Police Association (NBPA) put out a very strong statement saying:

"The National Black Police Association has championed for equality in the police service for over 20 years. Experience has shown us that the best way to undermine anti-racism is to seek out and actively involve those who don't recognise or understand it. This serves to provide legitimacy to strident views, steeped in the politics of division and is part of the backlash against the progression of racial equality which the NBPA has consistently warned.

It is difficult for the NBPA to welcome or endorse a report which to all intents and purposes includes a number of positive sections on policing. Sadly, these sections are rendered meaningless through a consistent problematisation of Black and Minority Ethnic Communities.

"As a police staff association which gave evidence to the Macpherson inquiry into the death of Stephen Lawrence in 1998, we are appalled that the Commission not only brazenly and wrongly stated that 'one of the key justifications for the Macpherson report's findings of institutional racism was the under reporting of racist crime'. It has mischievously stated that institutional racism in policing "is largely no longer the case given that hate crime and race related incidents are now widely reported by police forces". This is not the lived experience of our members, Black and Minority Ethnic police officers and staff and the diverse communities we serve.

"The NBPA would like to remind the Commission that in establishing and adopting the definition of institutional racism, the Macpherson inquiry did not restrict itself to hate crime and race related incidents. It also explored issues of police discipline, complaints, stop and search, selection, promotion, recruitment and retention. The NBPA is concerned that the commission has created a false and misleading narrative which will only serve to deepen mistrust and make our role harder."

In July 2020, I was interviewed by my local paper the *Swindon Advertiser* to highlight a call for public bodies to review equality policies in the wake of the brutal murder of George Floyd. I am now calling for all public bodies to review their equality policies. They need to review them with a special regard to RACE, which is still a taboo subject, starting with the seventy recommendations from the Macpherson Report. Although this Report led to the Race Relation Amendment Act in 2001, and public bodies being given a legal duty to promote race equality, most only paid lip service to it and in reality nothing much has changed.

Since 2010 we also have the Equality Act which covers the nine protected characteristics including, age, disability, gender, LGBT etc. However, from my experience, people will generally discuss things like disability and gender, which I hasten to add, are very important to people in these categories, but as soon as one mentions race others will go quiet or defensive. So race is still a taboo subject and remains one of the 'uncomfortable truths' that people prefer to shy away from.

Several Black workers in the public sector have told me that when race is mentioned it's quickly shut down by their colleagues and managers resulting in no opportunity to learn. To use a Jamaican proverbial saying: "who feels it knows it". If you have not lived or experienced it, how do you know what it's like?

We now know that there have been a disproportionate number of BAME deaths in the NHS due to Covid-19. I was a member of on an equality and advisory panel at the Great Western hospital in Swindon, which was subsequently disbanded. Re-opening this panel would be a good starting point.

COMMISSION ON RACE AND ETHNIC DISPARITIES (CRED) REPORT

Following the publication, in March 2021, of the much maligned Commission on Race and Ethnic Disparities (CRED) report, the National Church Leaders Forum (NCLF), 'a Black Christian voice', released the following statement on 6 April 2021: "Since the publication of the report, there have been widespread expressions of dissatisfaction with some of its contents, with some of our leaders expressing on behalf of their parishioners feelings of deep hurt, especially concerning the suggestion that institutional or systemic racism in the UK no longer exists. This runs counter to their lived experiences and the success of some has been achieved in spite of, not in the absence of, institutional or systemic racism. This miscalculation is to be regretted since it hinders real engagement with elements of the report that could be impactful."

The church leaders went on to say that while significant progress has been made in our multicultural society, much more needs to be done before the UK can justly regard itself as a beacon of racial justice in the world.

Despite the outcry, I agreed with the NCLF in that we need to move on and make positive changes. They said: "NCLF calls upon all participants in public discourse to adopt a respectful and constructive approach in the exchange of views. Church leaders stand ready to contribute to conversations and actions leading to a more racially and ethnically just country."

However, so far the strongest criticism came from Geneva on 19 April 2021. A group of UN human rights experts strongly rejected the UK government-backed report into racism and ethnic disparities in the country, saying that it further distorted and falsified historic facts, and could even fuel racism, racial discrimination and negative racial stereotypes.

According to the UN Working Group of Experts on People of African Descent, "In 2021, it is stunning to read a Report on race and ethnicity that repackages racist tropes and stereotypes into fact, twisting data and misapplying statistics and studies into conclusory findings and ad hominem attacks on people of African descent ... The Report cites dubious evidence to make claims that rationalise white supremacy by using the familiar arguments that have always justified racial hierarchy. This attempt to normalise white supremacy despite considerable research and evidence of institutional racism is an unfortunate sidestepping of the opportunity to acknowledge the atrocities of the past and the contributions of all in order to move forward."

In a further statement, the working group condemned the report's assertion that while there might be overt acts of racism in the UK, there was no institutional racism. "The report's conclusion that racism is either a product of the imagination of people of African descent or of discrete, individualised incidents ignores the pervasive role that the social construction of race was designed to play in society, particularly in normalising atrocity, in which the British state and institutions played a significant role."

The experts said the report omits any recognition or analysis of institutional racism by international human rights experts, including the UN Working Group of Experts on People of African Descent's 2012 review after its visit to the UK. Without exception, these reports have highlighted the damaging impact of institutional racism and deep-rooted inequities in areas such as health, education, employment, housing, stop-and-search practices, and the criminal justice system in the UK.

"The reality is that People of African descent continue to experience poor economic, social, and health outcomes at vastly disproportionate rates in the UK. While racial disparities may not always stem from racism or racial discrimination, there is also compelling evidence that the roots of these disparities lie in institutional racism and structural discrimination as they clearly do not reflect the preferences or priorities of the communities facing structural disadvantage."

At the time of concluding this book there was a petition of over 20,000 signatures calling for the withdrawal of the CRED Report. According to the critics, the main concern is the denial of the existence of institutional racism in the UK, which was categorically stated otherwise in the Macpherson Report into the murder of Stephen Lawrence.

Professor Gus John rightly said in the *Gleaner* newspaper on 15 April 2021 that Tony Sewell, who led the commission, is far too easy a target. Organising ourselves to use our power strategically and make sure the likes of Sewell are not imposed upon us, is even a more urgent task, and one into which we should be all putting our energy.

THE BAME ACRONYM

The commission recommended that the acronym BAME (Black, Asian and Minority Ethnic) should no longer be used, as differences between groups are as important as what they have in common. I partly agree with this.

Whilst working in local government some of my colleagues did not like the previous term BME, because the letter A for Asian was not included. As a result, people settled for BAME. However, this term can be misleading. For example, one could say an organisation has 20 per cent BAME staff, but only 2 per cent are from the African Caribbean community. This is no disrespect to other ethnic minorities, but it is not of much help when you are trying to be more specific.

VARIOUS REPORTS

Over the past forty years, there have been numerous reports, reviews and plans designed to tackle racism in our society. To name just a few: the Parker Review on the diversity on boards; the McGregor-Smith Review on race in the workplace; the Lammy Review on Black, Asian and Minority Ethnic (BAME) individuals in the criminal justice system; and Theresa May's Race Disparity Audit which focused on data by ethnicity. However, they have all been to no avail, as implementation of the recommendations contained in them is woefully inadequate and these reports gather dust on the shelves.

Gary Douglas, a journalist from *The Voice* newspaper came to interview me at my home in Swindon. In the 1 August 2005 edition, under the subsequent article's headline, 'A man for all people', he wrote that "Activist Steve Stephenson has dedicated his life to his community". This really is no exaggeration, and I will be happy to also be remembered as a person who *did* make a difference.

POSSIBLE SOLUTIONS

We need to continue the momentum created by the tragic killing of George Floyd. The systemic, structural racism towards Black people must be acknowledged and action taken to combat it. Equality and, particularly, racial equality measures must be part of the mainstream and not an 'add on' or afterthought. Institutions need to stop hiding behind the terms 'equality and diversity' which have been used to divert attention from looking at individual and institutional racism. We need to bring into force, in a meaningful way, Section 1 of the Equality Act 2010 in relation to the Public Sector Equality Duty.

I wholeheartedly endorse comments made by Helen Grant MP for Maidstone: "In both the private and public sector I would like to see compulsory data collection and disclosure relating to BAME recruitment, retention, promotion and pay."

I also strongly believe that all public bodies should have an equality duty in all job descriptions, which should be linked to promotion, and no annual increments should be paid if the actions in the duty are not met. All forms of race and equality training should be mandatory during induction and reviewed every six months.

Engagement with 'grass roots' Black and minority ethnic communities needs to be effective. In our community we also need to be more proactive. Over the years, I have experienced many individuals who approached me with a lot of good ideas, which need to be implemented. I usually advised the individual or organisation to take the lead on their proposals, and I will support them. The response was often that they don't have the time or the knowhow. I maintain that people will never gain the skills or knowledge if you are not prepared to go the extra mile.

We also need to have honest discussions with ourselves about where we are as a community. We can't blame others for everything that happens to us. When I was manager at the Malcolm X Community Centre in St Pauls, Bristol, I had an interview with BBC Radio Bristol in January 2016. I made the following comments when the council announced that they were planning to terminate the tenancy of the

Malcom X Community Centre: "[There was a] perception in the community that race plays a part in the decisions … I would say that we need to get our house in order – there are things we need to do that don't have anything to do with race."

Whilst there are always underlying issues about race, at times we need to have look at ourselves as a community, and engage in honest conversations.

Finally, I would like to end with a quote from Nelson Mandela, former president of South Africa:

"What counts in life is not the mere fact that we have lived. It is what difference we have made to the lives of others that will determine the significance of the life we lead."

Following the above comments in this book, "Are we not the children of the same god?"

Awards and Honours

With the support of my wife Pamela, and our daughters, Andrea and Simone when they were old enough, I have continuously raised money with my initiatives and assisted many individuals and organisations. For example: I was patron of Cornwall College and Montego Bay High School, alongside Derek Heaven, High Commissioner of Jamaica, and set up their events at Campbell Park in Milton Keynes. This organisation, of which my friend Wain McIntosh was also a member of the committee, raised thousands of pounds before eventually closing down.

Over many years, I acquired and then donated many autographed photos, cricket bats and footballs. I donated a West Indies cricket bat to Josephine Williams of Jamaica Basic Schools which raised £600, and two bats to Angela Christian of the Angel Foundation which raised a similar amount. Angela told me that she bought blood pressure machines for Jamaica with that money. I gave a signed Chelsea football which Paul Elliott had donated to a youth club in Oakley, Bedfordshire, which raised a substantial sum. I took fifty young people from the youth club on a coach trip to Aston Villa football club and meet the footballers outside the players' lounge.

I want to, once again, pay a special tribute to my wife Pamela for her unconditional love and support, without which none of these awards and honours would have been possible. My daughters have also contributed to these achievements, having assisted at many of the events and especially with the West Indies cricket team.

FRIENDS OF THE CARIBBEAN SPECIAL AWARD, 2019

This award was presented to me at an event in Milton Keynes, by the Rev. Rose Hudson Wilkins, former Queen's chaplain and former chaplain to the Speaker of the House of Commons, who is now the Bishop of Dover, and Wain McIntosh, Chair of the Friends of the Caribbean. This was a great honour because both Wain and Rose have become two of our best role models. I later became equality officer on a voluntary basis for the organisation.

MOBO AWARD NOMINATION, 2015

I was nominated for a MOBO (Music of Black Origin) Award in 2015. Although I did not receive the main award in the community category I was very pleased to be recognised. I was also delighted that a young man involved in the fight against knife crime won the award.

LUTON HIDDEN CREATIVE ECONOMY AWARD, 2015

I received this award for my work in Luton in Bedfordshire.

BIRMINGHAM HIDDEN CREATIVE ECONOMY AWARD, 2013

I received this award for my voluntary work in Birmingham.

JAMAICA'S 50TH ANNIVERSARY OF INDEPENDENCE SPECIAL AWARD FOR SERVICES TO SPORTS, 2012

I received this award at the Arsenal Emirates football stadium in London. This was an important and special award for me. Two of my friends were also nominated: Al Hamilton, the founder the Commonwealth Sports Award and the late Sted Wallen, founder of the Malcolm Marshall Memorial Match. Over the years we have supported each other and my respect goes out to both Al and Sted. Two of my idols were also present at the event: Donald Quarrie and Merlyn Ottey, both great Jamaican Olympic champions.

I was especially pleased to see Don again because we had both attended Camperdown High School in Kingston. Whilst living in Birmingham, I once went to the Alexander Stadium, where Don was a guest, because my daughter Andrea wanted his autograph. She did not believe that I would be able to get it, but I simply walked up to the track side and shouted, "DQ, DQ". He looked around as he figured it was someone from Jamaica who knew one of his nicknames, and duly signed the programme to Andrea's delight.

PRIME MINISTER'S MEDAL FOR SERVICES TO JAMAICA AND THE CARIBBEAN, 2003

Whilst the MBE was a major achievement, this award from Jamaica was the icing on the cake. And receiving it was one of the highlights of my work for the Caribbean community. Having just returned from Jamaica in July 2003, I received a large brown envelope from the Jamaican government. The letter stated that I was the recipient of the Prime Minister's Medal from P.J. Patterson, the then prime minister of Jamaica. I told my wife Pamela that I was greatly honoured and surprised by this international award, but would not be going back to Jamaica for the ceremony, which was in a few weeks' time. Pamela insisted upon paying the air fare, saying that this was a once in a lifetime event, and she reminded me of all the help and support I had given to Jamaica since the hurricane in 1979. One of the things that she was most proud of was when I presented five new wheelchairs to Major Desmond Clarke at the St Joseph Golden Age home in Kingston.

As a result of this award, I was paid a compliment by the CEO of Swindon Borough Council, who came to see me and said that with so many bad news stories around he had instructed the director of communications to write an article, with photos taken in the gardens of the civic office. He also gave me permission take time off from work to attend the ceremony in Jamaica.

Receiving the Prime Minister's Medal from Jamaica's Prime Minister, PJ Patterson, at the Jamaican High Commission in London in 2003.

The ceremony was a very proud moment in my life, not just for me but my beloved Aunt Eda who also attended. She was so proud to be sitting there with me, the prime minister and other dignitaries and community representatives from the USA and Canada.

A recipient from the USA noted that I was one of the youngest recipients, and said that I must have been helping the community in England and Jamaica for a long time. He was right.

My long-time friend Courtney Walsh, who supported many of my charity events, also attended the ceremony at Independence Park. Courtney had come to take me out for dinner and a drink, but by the time he arrived I had already left. However, we met up the next day to celebrate my achievement. Courtney felt very proud because he has witnessed and participated in a lot of my work, and he had seen what I was doing in the UK.

I was pleased to receive a special letter of congratulations from Brian Breese, the CEO of the Jamaica Cricket Board. A lot of the cricket gear I sent to Jamaica had been passed to Brian for sharing out to the cricketers who were doing an excellent job.

A few months later I was talking to Trevor Taylor, manager of Victoria Mutual Building Society in the UK, and he congratulated me with a big smile on his face. Trevor said, "You remember when I told you VM in Jamaica wanted a profile of you. This was not for VM; it was Mrs Delores Cooper from the High Commission who requested the profile to be sent to the Jamaican Government."

THE VOICE NEWSPAPER, SPECIAL RACE RELATIONS AWARD, 1998

I received this award at the Grosvenor Hotel in London alongside Neville Lawrence, father of murdered teenager Stephen Lawrence, who received the Special Community

With Neville Lawrence, father of the murdered teenager, Stephen Lawrence, in 1998 after receiving our awards from *The Voice* newspaper.

Award. This was my second award from *The Voice*, and was given in the presence of a host of celebrity guests like boxers Frank Bruno and Lennox Lewis, and friends such as actress Donna Croll.

I recall a photo on the front of *The Voice* with my friend and colleague Bert Cuff, who received an award for his work in Northamptonshire, along with Diane Abbott, Baroness Ros Howells and Brenda Emmanus, to name but a few. I noted Bert was given another special award at a local reception in Northampton, which was well deserved.

MBE, 1996

The MBE was my fifth award, and some of my friends said they were not surprised because they felt it was a natural progression towards such recognition. It was a brilliant day at Buckingham Palace with Pamela, Andrea and Simone, the three beautiful ladies in my life. For Pamela, it was some compensation for all the late night community meetings I used to attend as well as running the Saturday club at the Starlight. This had usually been followed by a dance in the evening, meaning that I did not return home until the early hours of Sunday morning.

My friend Zahid Ali from the *Caribbean Times* was outside the gates of Buckingham Palace and took photos that were put on the front page of that publication. I am forever grateful to him for doing this.

As a sports person, I was pleased to see footballer Neville Southall, golfer Sam Torrance, and the late motor racing commentator Murray Walker. They were all receiving awards on that day.

There was an incident that day that relates directly to the 'Black Lives Matter' campaign. My younger daughter Simone was standing waiting for us, whilst a well-dressed lady was looking around. The lady handed her coat to Simone assuming that this young Black girl was an employee at Buckingham Palace. To this day, such incidents of racial stereotyping are not uncommon.

At Buckingham Palace with my wife, Pamela, after receiving the MBE for services to the community in Bedfordshire in the Queen's Birthday Honours in 1996. Photo: Zahid Ali / Hansib

My wife Pamela had a similar, but more upsetting experience at a hotel in Bristol. The night before it occurred we had been at a dinner and reception in the presence of Derek Heaven, the then High Commissioner of Jamaica, and Captain Horace Burrell, chair of the Jamaica Football Federation. Pamela was in the lift with a white woman who turned and asked her if she was one of the cleaners because water had been spilled and she wanted it cleaned up. Pamela was very upset and we complained to the hotel reception.

I was further honoured at an award celebration that Pamela had arranged at the Five O Caribbean Club in

Luton. At the time, it was one of the largest such events in Luton. My friend Rudolph Walker from the TV soap *EastEnders* attended and paid tribute to me, as well as many other friends.

It is now more common for members of the Black, Asian and minority ethnic community to receive such honours from the Queen, but in 1996 it was not so. Hence the big celebrations in Luton! On the Monday after the event, I was in the town centre and saw Dave, one of the owners of the club. He had a big smile on his face, and told me that he had to open the club's third bar, which was usually closed, and almost sold out all the drinks. I was humbled and pleased to have played a part in swelling the coffers of this essential community hub.

THE VOICE NEWSPAPER AWARD, 1995

The Voice newspaper award was my fourth award and was given to me in London by the editor, Winsome Cornish.

CITIZENSHIP AWARD FROM THE CRE & THE INSTITUTE OF CITIZENSHIP STUDIES, 1995

I received the citizenship award in the highly commended category from the Commission for Racial Equality (CRE) and the Institute of Citizenship Studies at a ceremony in Manchester. I was not feeling well on the day as I had the flu, but my wife felt that I needed to make the effort to attend. I had worked very hard over the years, attending many community meetings and arriving home late at night at least twice a week, as well as working full time as principal officer ethnic minorities for Northamptonshire Social Services.

The BBC's Martin Lewis presented the award in the presence of Lord Weatherall, the Chair of the Institute for Citizenship Studies, and Herman Ouseley, a person I had admired for many years, and who was the chair of the CRE. During the ceremony it was revealed that there were 171 nominations and I had finished third.

Pictured with my Citizenship Award in 1995 with, from left, the BBC's Martin
Lewis, Herman Ouseley and Lord Weatherhill.

This national award was important in the sense that it
was my first award from what we would call the
'mainstream'. All my other awards were from Black-led
organisations, except the MBE.

Herman told me afterwards that he was very
disappointed that the mainstream press had not seen it fit
to cover the event. Had it been an occasion with any hint of
controversy or negativity, especially where the Black
community was concerned, he felt that the media would
have been there in their droves!

THE GLEANER NEWSPAPER MERIT AWARD, 1993

This was presented to me at a ceremony in London. Bill
Morris, general secretary of the Transport and General
Workers' Union, received the main award for his trade union
work. I was pleased to be in such illustrious company.

HANSIB COMMUNITY AWARD LONDON 1991

In 1991, I received the Hansib Community Award from Arif
Ali of Hansib Publications (publishers of the *Caribbean
Times* newspaper). After the Cobra Award, I received a call

from Arif who stated that from what he had seen of my voluntary work in Luton, and the work I had done with young people, I should receive one of their community awards.

I told him that since being in Birmingham I could not have been so successful with my sports and charity work without help from Cyrille Regis, whom I called the 'doyen of Black British footballers'. Arif, who admired Cyrille for his skills on the pitch, had no problem in also awarding Cyrille with a Hansib Community Award at an event held at the Wembley Conference Centre.

COBRA AWARD, 1990

I received this award at Luton Town Hall where it was presented by Arif Ali, editor of the *Caribbean Times*. I think this was a befitting award for all my voluntary work in Luton. I had re-opened the Starlight Youth Club using my own money in June 1980, and had just returned from Birmingham where my voluntary work with the support of Cyrille Regis, Paul Elliott and Mark Walters, had flourished. It was nice to be recognised by my community because a lot of people that I met in the town whenever I visited mentioned how much I was missed after leaving in 1986.

TESTIMONIAL FROM THE CHIEF CONSTABLE OF BEDFORDSHIRE POLICE, 1981

The testimonial from Andrew Sloan, the chief constable of Bedfordshire Police, was for helping to restore the peace in Luton after the racially-charged disturbances in 1981.